BUTTONS

BUTTONS
A Collector's Guide

by
Victor Houart

CHARLES SCRIBNER'S SONS
NEW YORK

EB HT JO MW

Book designed by Pamela Mara

Printed in Great Britain
Library of Congress Catalog Card Number 77–79904
ISBN 0–684–15334–3

1 3 5 7 9 11 13 15 17 19 I/C 20 18 16 14 12 10 8 6
4 2

ACKNOWLEDGMENTS

FIRST, my grateful thanks to Stephen Price, of the Birmingham City Museums and Art Gallery, who, with the blessing of John Ruffle, keeper of the Department of Archaeology, sent me valuable information and allowed me to look through the many documents related to the Birmingham button industry of the past which he had assembled. Many thanks also to Mme Préaud, of the Manufacture Nationale de Sèvres, M. Le Barazer, of the Etablissements Parent-Corona in Paris, who went out of his way to help, and Mr McGregor, of the Royal Air Force Museum in Hendon, for information received.

Thanks as well to the following persons for giving me photographs: Miss Judith Turner, London public relations officer of Josiah Wedgwood and Sons Ltd; Mr W. H. Fisher, of Royal Doulton Tableware Ltd; and M. Wittamer, of Brussels, who owns a very complete button collection.

And finally I want to thank my friend Peter Glover, for checking my manuscript, and my wife Margaret, who brought home so many beautiful buttons.

Victor Houart
September 1976

FOREWORD

THE hobby of collecting buttons is still a new one, but it is rapidly gaining popularity. Enthusiasts are already engaged in serious research, and hitherto unknown buttons are turning up all the time, for buttons have been manufactured by the billion all over the world. But the would-be collector should be warned that, if he wants to put together a worthwhile collection, he has to be very selective. This principle applies of course to any form of collecting: bad and indifferent pieces have been made in any period of history, and only the best is worth saving for the future. It is pointless therefore to hoard cheap shirt or trouser buttons, or even reproductions of ancient buttons, none of which will ever have a commercial value or take the fancy of the true connoisseur. The buttons in a collection must be genuinely antique, and it is pointless to waste money on reproductions. In fact, with one or two very rare exceptions, the latest period for European buttons worth collecting is that of the Art Nouveau designs, which ceased to be produced after 1910. The exceptions are original buttons made after 1910 but which are connected with some historical event or have a commemorative purpose: or those which have an unmistakable style, such as the Art Deco buttons and those rather amusing glass realistics made for children in the 1930s.

This guide, organised alphabetically according to manufacturer, the material from which the buttons are made, or the themes they represent, concentrates upon European buttons—perhaps particularly the French and English ones, the most beautiful ever made. Japan, India, the Middle East and the United States all yield fine craftsman-made buttons for the collector however.

One final thought—true appreciation comes only from increasing knowledge, the product of time and application. In return for these two, a fascinating and worthwhile hobby can be open to anyone, at relatively little cost.

ACORN BUTTONS

BUTTONS in the shape of acorns, or made from real acorns, were to be found in many places during the nineteenth century, but mainly in Germany. Sometimes other nuts were used, with shanks attached to them. Imitation acorn buttons were made of wood and painted. Hazel-nut buttons were made in Germany until about 1950. They are all curiosities rather than collectors' items.

19th-century acorn button in painted wood.

AGATE BUTTONS

AGATE is a variety of quartz, one of the chalcedonies, which also include other semi-precious stones such as cornelian and onyx. Its colours are arranged in concentric rings and therefore some stones, if cut downwards, appear to have stripes.

Imitation agate buttons decorated with glass. Probably used on fur coats. 19th century.

The first known agate buttons were made during the eighteenth century on a very limited scale, most of the early specimens being composed of a highly polished agate disc mounted on a metallic rim fitted with a pin shank. The few agate buttons made in the nineteenth century and at the beginning of the twentieth were usually constructed of simple pieces of agate cut in different shapes, sometimes fitted with a pin shank, sometimes with a shank plate at the back, leaving the stone entirely free of decoration; though a few, produced during the nineteenth century, were small and decorated with pieces of agate mounted in claws. This type of button is by no means easy to find.

ALLEN AND MOORE

THIS firm of English buttonmakers founded their factory at 36 Great Hampton Road, Birmingham in 1855. There is no record of it after 1870, when the firm presumably either moved or was taken over. Its production was mainly limited to metal buttons for the Royal Navy and the British Army.

ALUMINIUM BUTTONS

MOST aluminium buttons were manufactured in the United States and did not cross the Atlantic. Mainly produced at the end of the nineteenth century, their production was limited by the fact that aluminium at the time was as precious as silver. Some buttons were covered with a coat of lacquer which could be engraved. Production was resumed on a limited scale in the 1930s.

ANIMAL DESIGNS

Picture button with lion design.

BUTTON makers all over the world have often found inspiration in the animal kingdom. The practice started in the eighteenth century, when the first hunting buttons were produced in France and England. Designs of animals, both wild and domestic, were at first engraved on silver or brass, or painted on enamel; but most buttons decorated with animal designs date from the second half of the nineteenth century when the stamped picture button became fashionable. Almost every animal has been portrayed in this way. The most popular were horses, dogs, deer, boar, cows and foxes, but a collector may well come across representations of bats, rats, elephants and lions.

Animal designs are also found on enamel, glass and horn sporting jewellery buttons of the nineteenth and twentieth centuries, some very interesting ones being painted on wood or applied by transfer on plastic buttons during the two decades preceding the Second World War.

Stamped metal buttons with animal designs. 19th century.

ARCHAL BUTTONS

THESE metal buttons were manufactured in Europe throughout the Middle Ages and were referred to in many ancient documents, but none are known to have survived. 'Archal' was a metal alloy in extensive use for two or three centuries, but its composition still remains something of a mystery. It probably contained copper or bronze, and owes its name to a certain Richard Archal, the French inventor of a draw-plate.

ARCHITECTURAL DESIGNS

ARCHITECTURAL structures of all kinds have been a source of inspiration for button designers for more than two centuries. Buildings, from small cottages to huge palaces, have been reproduced on buttons, some of them actual buildings which existed at the time of manufacture. The most attractive buttons of this type

Set of five 19th-century buttons depicting various architectural designs. Four are stamped metal, the fifth (top right) is celluloid mounted on metal.

11

were produced in Paris in the last quarter of the eighteenth century, during the Louis XVI period. The set of sixteen under-glass buttons, each decorated with an engraving of a different Paris monument, is well known among collectors.

Although most of the structures reproduced on buttons were actual buildings, it is not now possible to identify all of them. The easy ones are the Eiffel Tower, the Cathedral of Nôtre-Dame, the Statue of Liberty, the Masonic Temple in Chicago and the church of Sacre-Coeur in Montmartre. Some others, such as Greek and Roman

19th-century stamped
metal picture buttons with
architectural designs.

19th-century stamped metal picture buttons with architectural designs.

temples, Chinese pagodas, old bridges, mountain cottages and Dutch windmills, may well have been inspired by drawings, engravings or paintings. Architectural designs appear mainly on nineteenth-century picture buttons, but they are also found moulded, carved, printed, and engraved, on glass, enamel, horn, ivory, wood, and plastic buttons.

German picture button: a chalet in the Alps.

French picture button: Paris monuments.

14

ARMFIELD AND CO. LTD.

THIS firm, founded in Holloway Park, Birmingham, in 1763, specialised from the start in making brass buttons for the Royal Navy and the British army. These buttons were much valued for their fine designs, and Nelson is said to have worn Armfield buttons on his uniform at the Battle of Trafalgar. When the business outgrew the factory in 1790, Armfield moved it to Newhall Street. In 1891 a further move took place, to St Paul's Square, where it was completely demolished by the bombings of 1940.

It is known that around 1850 Edward Armfield had as partner a certain Charles Frederick Perkin. When Armfield died in 1870, Perkin took over the business and became its owner in 1911, using the name Charles Armfield Perkin. His son Alfred, born in Birmingham in 1877, was attached to the firm in 1915 and his grandson, Clifford Armfield Perkin, worked for the firm from 1927, and became a director in 1940.

ART NOUVEAU BUTTONS

THE radical Art Nouveau movement within the decorative arts, which flourished around the end of the last century and the

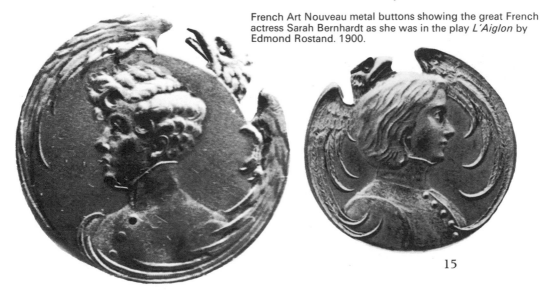

French Art Nouveau metal buttons showing the great French actress Sarah Bernhardt as she was in the play *L'Aiglon* by Edmond Rostand. 1900.

15

English Art Nouveau silver button with the Birmingham hallmark for 1902.

Beautiful French Art Nouveau buttons in stamped metal. 1900.

beginning of this, really comprised a variety of styles whose common denominator was the desire to be new. Novelty became an internationally accepted ideal in itself, but much attention was also paid to the design of everyday objects from a teapot to a simple light-fitting. Women were depicted in drawings, carvings and paintings, as strange solemn beings with strong jaws, dramatic eyes and an abundance of wavy hair. Inspiration was found in ancient or foreign cultures, and Celtic and Japanese motifs were used. These trends are reflected in buttons manufactured during the period. Art Nouveau buttons are classified by collectors into three categories: (1) those decorated with abstract motifs, (2) those decorated with flowing floral designs, or heads and busts of typical Art Nouveau women and (3) buttons decorated with geometrical abstract designs or Celtic-inspired designs. Some of these beautiful buttons are made in silver, but most of them in stamped metal. The great French actress, Sarah Bernhardt, is often represented on them, the designs inspired by the drawings of Mucha.

Art Nouveau buttons.

French Art Nouveau buttons. 1900.

16

ASTON, WILLIAM

ASTON was an English buttonmaker whose Birmingham firm had many commercial successes between the second quarter of the nineteenth century and 1876, when its name disappeared from the Birmingham directories. The Aston firm, which employed between 700 and 800 people, was located at 33/37 Princip Street. The three-fold linen button, which William Aston had patented, was actually invented for him by his friend Humphrey Jeffreys, a well-known Midlands character, famous for his experiments with kites and balloons.

AVENTURINE BUTTONS

AVENTURINE, sometimes called goldstone, is a rather opaque, yellowish-brown quartz speckled with very tiny golden flecks. Buttons decorated with the real stone are not known to exist, but quite a number of buttons decorated with a glass imitation known as aventurine glass, can be found. This glass is made by throwing copper at random (in French, '*à l'aventure*', hence its name), into molten glass. In fact aventurine glass, which was manufactured for a long time at Murano in Italy, existed before the stone was discovered in the middle of the nineteenth century. The buttons are either fitted with a metal shank or with four holes for sewing. Some nineteenth-century jewelled buttons have an aventurine glass centre.

AVIATION BUTTONS

AVIATION does not seem to have been a very great source of inspiration to the buttonmakers, if one disregards the millions of buttons which have been manufactured, mainly in brass, for the airlines and the air forces of the world. Some cheap modern buttons have aviation motifs, but they are not really collectors' items. However, a beautiful and now very rare aviation button was made by an unknown French firm in 1909, on which the famous aircraft *11 bis* is represented. In that aircraft Louis Blériot flew the Channel for the first time. Although balloons appear on many buttons (see Balloon Buttons), nobody seems to have thought about using airship designs.

BACK MARKS

NO button bearing a back-mark stamped on its reverse side can be older that the beginning of the nineteenth century, when such marks first appeared. Occasionally marks allow collectors to determine with some degree of accuracy the period of production, but only when the history of the firm has been firmly and accurately established. Mostly the back-marks simply help to establish the country of origin.

(See Patent Office Registration mark)

BADDELEY

BADDELEY was probably the earliest buttonmaker of Birmingham. The history of his firm remains rather obscure but it is known that his workshop was in Old Square, Birmingham, and that he retired from business in 1739. According to Birmingham tradition he invented various machine-tools designed to speed up button production methods.

BALLOON BUTTONS

IMMEDIATELY after the successful ascent of the Montgolfier

18

brothers in the very first hot-air balloon, on 4th June 1783, beautiful buttons *à la Mongolfière* appeared in various Paris boutiques. They were followed very soon after by buttons *au ballon* after the first ascent of a hydrogen-filled balloon, on 27th August of the same year. Eighteenth-century balloon buttons are very rare and prized possessions today. They are all underglass in copper frames, decorated with various views of balloon ascents reproduced in paint on silk or paper, or by engravings on paper.

The production of such buttons did not cease in 1786 when the balloon craze died down, but continued into the early years of the nineteenth century. Copies have been made ever since, mainly in France. A very few balloon buttons exist with scenes etched on burnished steel, but they are practically unobtainable.

BASSOT, EMILE

BASSOT was a French buttonmaker active at the beginning of the nineteenth century, and famous in France for his stamped horn buttons. It is known that he requested a patent in 1830 to protect their manufacture. The hunting buttons produced by his firm are called Bassot buttons. (See Horn Buttons)

BATTERSEA BUTTONS

A FAMOUS London enamel factory, located at York House, Battersea, was founded in July 1753 by a certain Stephen-Theodore Janssen. It achieved a fame which far exceeded the short years of its actual existence. In three years, Battersea produced what is considered the very best in transfer-decorated enamels. Janssen had two partners, John Brooks and Henry Delamain, both of Irish origin. It is thought that it was John Brooks who invented the process of transfer printing which was subsequently adopted by the English ceramic industry. The fact that such small articles as buttons were made at Battersea is known from notices printed at the time of Janssen's bankruptcy in 1756, when his stock was sold at auction. It has been so far impossible to identify buttons made at Battersea, for many other enamel buttons, probably of similar type, were produced in Birmingham and South Staffordshire. A Battersea enamel button would be a prize possession.

BERGEROT

BERGEROT was a French buttonmaker active at the end of the eighteenth century in Paris. His button shop was in the Rue de Betisy, in the Maison Montbazon. He had the reputation of being one of the first French button-makers to have produced buttons on a wide scale instead of producing sets one at a time, as had been the practice up to that time.

BERLIN IRON BUTTONS

WHEN, in times of peace, German armourers had to stop making helmets, shields and the like, they converted their factories to the manufacture of other iron implements. The industry started in the seventeenth century, mainly in the region of Silesia. But the first factory to produce only iron jewellery was the Royal Berlin Factory, founded in 1804. It was captured by French troops in 1806 and all the moulds were brought to France. Later, other factories in Berlin resumed the manufacture of small objects such as iron crosses, shoe buckles, bracelets, brooches, fans and buttons. The last Berlin iron jewellery was produced between 1850 and 1860. Much Berlin jewellery has now found its way into collections, but buttons are very rare.

BERNHARDT, SARAH

THE famous French actress was born in Paris in 1844. She joined the Comédie Française in 1872 and was an immediate success. In 1898 she rented the Théâtre des Nations, which became known as the Sarah Bernhardt Theatre, and there she put on the Edmond Rostand play L'Aiglon (The Eaglet). The event was recorded on metal buttons at the time. These buttons, which are not rare, are decorated with the bust of Sarah Bernhardt, dressed in the Austrian uniform of Napoléon's son. Other, more cheaply made buttons show only her head, the design taken from the drawings of Mucha.

BICYCLE BUTTONS

ALL types of bicycles are represented on metal buttons manufactured at the end of the nineteenth century. Some are also painted on enamel or engraved on metal. European buttonmakers, however, paid less attention to the bicycle than their American colleagues. A number of American bicycle firms produced bicycle buttons, mostly for advertising purposes. The League of American Wheelmen issued several types, in enamel, with at least one advertising a tandem.

BIRDS

BIRDS have been among the favourite subjects of buttonmakers of all times and all countries. They were represented on all types of buttons in the eighteenth and nineteenth centuries, but it is sometimes rather difficult to identify the birds as some are of fanciful design. Birds appeared on under-glass, *eglomisé* and reverse-painting buttons in the eighteenth century. They were also painted on ivory and on wood and moulded in glass. They appear on countless picture buttons of the second half of the nineteenth century. Among the many identifiable birds are owls, peacocks, eagles, pheasants, swallows, swans, pigeons, flamingoes and herons.

Set of metal picture buttons showing various birds. These buttons were manufactured between 1880 and the beginning of the first world war.

French brass buttons
with bird designs.

BOIS DURCI BUTTONS

BOIS durci (hardened, or plastic wood) was an ancestor of the modern plastics. The substance was invented by Charles Lepage of Paris around 1855, but the first manufacturer was a certain Latry, also of Paris. The material, very hard and non-inflammable, consisted of a combination of sawdust and albumen from eggs or blood, which could be moulded. Many objects have been made with *bois durci* in bronze or jetblack colours, such as snuff boxes, picture frames, dominoes, brooches, combs, necklaces and cameo-type médallions. Buttons made in *bois durci* are usually of the cameo type, with an impression in relief depicting a head, most often that of a woman.

Bois durci buttons, although quite rare, do not fetch high prices.

BONE BUTTONS

BONE buttons were probably the earliest to be manufactured in Europe. There is documentary evidence that the Parisian *paternôt-riers* (rosary-makers) of the twelfth century were already making them. Bone buttons, unless they are heavily decorated, are not sought after by collectors as they are rather dull. Billions of them were made during the eighteenth and nineteenth centuries to fasten shirts, underwear and men's trousers. Those made in the eighteenth century are pierced with five holes instead of the usual four holes of today. Only about the middle of the nineteenth century did certain bone buttons come to be engraved, carved and inlaid with different materials. Bone buttons mounted on metal are rare. The main French centres for the manufacture of bone buttons were the little town of Meru (Seine et Oise), and a few villages along the lower Loire valley.

BOULTON, MATTHEW

BOULTON, a famous English industrialist of the eighteenth century, is reported to be, among other things, the inventor of the steel and the cut-steel buttons. His father was a maker of fancy goods, then called 'toys', mainly buckles and buttons. Young Matthew inherited his father's business in 1759. He soon outgrew his father's old premises in Birmingham and built a factory, the Soho Works, in Staffordshire, between 1759 and 1766. The Boulton factories produced billions of buttons of all types during the eighteenth century: gilt buttons, silver-plated buttons, buttons inlaid with steel, buttons made of pinchbeck, hard white metal, fancy compositions, mother-of-pearl, polished steel and jettina, silver and gold, copper and enamel. The Museum of Sciences in Birmingham has several catalogues of the Boulton firm, and many of its buttons (which were sent all over the world) can be identified. It would have been Matthew Boulton senior who had the idea of replacing diamonds by the now famous cut-steels. That was around 1745. In 1773, Boulton ordered cameos in jasper-ware from his friend Josiah Wedgwood, mounted them in steel frames and thereby produced some of the most attractive buttons in the world. It is thought that he also used black basalt supplied by Wedgwood to decorate his buttons.

BREADALBANE BUTTONS

THE Breadalbane buttons were made by the famous makers of souvenir woodware, William Smith (1795–1847) and Andrew Smith (1797–1869), of Mauchline in Scotland. The Smiths' business apparently started in 1810, and in 1829 it had reached such a size that the two brothers opened a shop and showroom in Birmingham. The partnership ceased in 1843 and Andrew moved to 139 Great Charles Street, Birmingham. It is not known when the brothers started making buttons, but in 1847 Andrew was already advertising them in the Birmingham Directory, announcing that Breadalbane buttons were being produced under the patronage of H.R.H. Prince Albert. The advertisement adds 'Andrew Smith, inventor of the Breadalbane or Scotch wood button, begs to intimate to the trade that he commences the season with a great variety of new patterns and with a stock which will ensure the prompt supply of their orders. This button gives entire satisfaction in the durability of wear and firmness of shank, while for lightness, beauty and variety of ornament, it exceeds anything that has been made.' The Breadalbane buttons, named after the Marquis of Breadalbane, were made in sycamore wood and fitted with a cloth shank. They were all decorated, in three price ranges, with pen and ink pictures, tartans and transfers. As business boomed, Andrew appointed agents in London and in Paris and the export of tartan buttons became an important part of the firm's business. The process, of course, had become mechanised: the tartans were printed on paper which was then glued to the wood. Tartan-ware was made by the Smiths at least until the end of the nineteenth century.

BREAST-SHAPED BUTTONS

SILVER buttons fashioned after the female breast, and sometimes decorated with geometrical designs, were produced for more than two hundred years, up to the end of the nineteenth century. They were made mainly in Holland and Norway. It is interesting to note that the very first antique money boxes were manufactured in the same shape in the Mediterranean countries. The Dutch and Norwegian buttons of this type arc often hallmarked.

Norwegian breast-shaped button bearing the Bergen hallmark for 1863.

BRITANNIA METAL BUTTONS

BRITANNIA metal is a leadless alloy of tin and regulus of antimony, resembling silver or polished pewter in appearance. It was used in Great Britain from about 1770 well into the nineteenth century. As it is difficult to tell whether or not a button is made according to the 'right' formula, a collector can only put all white metal alloy buttons into one general category.

25

BRITISH BUTTONMAKING FIRMS

IN order to help collectors to identify the origin of some of their buttons by their backmark or their initials, a list of nineteenth-century British buttonmaking firms, and the materials in which they worked, is given below:

In Birmingham

Edward Banks—mother-of-pearl.

Chatwind and Son—black and white mother-of-pearl, gilt, glass, bronze and horn.

Hardman and Illiffe—military and passementerie.

Healey, James and Son—steel.

Ingram T. Well—horn.

Knowles H.—gilt, enamel.

Piggott and Co.—military and livery, gold and silver, glass and sporting.

Rawley, Charles—military and livery.

In London

Edwards, Robert—enamelled gold.

Philipps Bros.—gold and silver, decorated with rubies, turquoise and opal gems.

In Aberdeen

Jameson, George—granite.

There were other very important firms operating in the middle of the nineteenth century, but the precise nature of their production has never been ascertained. They are:

(1) Barwell
(2) Beck and Thomas
(3) Bratt and Cole
(4) Deakin
(5) Duncombe
(6) Egginton and Bingley
(7) Lesdam

BROCADE BUTTONS

BROCADE, from the Italian word 'brocatto', is a fabric embossed with silk, gold or silver thread, the motifs in relief. Brocade buttons were produced in the middle of the nineteenth century, when the manufacturers of this fabric produced large pieces decorated with small round patterns which could be cut out and mounted on metal frames. These buttons, always of rather drab colours, are not very popular.

BUFFALO BUTTONS

THIS is the name given by French buttonmakers to a certain type of button made by slicing small circular discs from antlers. Cut and polished, they retain the appearance and hardness of natural horn. Most buffalo buttons were made in Austria and Bavaria.

BUFFON BUTTONS

THE buttons called *à la Buffon* are probably among the rarest today. They were made in Paris during the last half of the eighteenth century, following the publication by Georges-Louis Leclerc, Comte de Buffon, of his book on natural history. The book met with an enormous success and in 1760, the buttonmakers began to bring out these very attractive underglass buttons, on which domed glass covered tiny insects, dried herbs and even tiny chips of stones. Sometimes called HABITAT BUTTONS.

18th-century underglass Buffon buttons mounted on copper. The insects, small stones and dried herbs were placed under the domed glass more than 200 years ago and are still in good condition.

BUTTONS LIMITED

BUTTONS Ltd was a firm founded in Birmingham in 1907 by the merger of Plant, Green and Manton Ltd, Thomas Carlyle Ltd and Harrison and Smith Ltd. The first president of the new firm was John R. Green. Until the merger took place, the future of the three small factories in Birmingham was uncertain and the company was formed

27

to cut the cost of production by closing the smaller works and concentrating production in larger factories. The business was thus enabled to compete more effectively with foreign producers. Right from the beginning, the materials used by Buttons Ltd were as varied as its production. The firm produced buttons made of pearl, steel, ivory, brass and other metals, buffalo horn, braid, leather, marble, enamel, coral, rock-crystal, jet, earthenware, porcelain and corozo.

Buttons Ltd owned three factories, in Warstone Street, Clissold Street and, the most important, in Portland Street.

The enterprise still exists in Birmingham today, as a division of Francis Summer Engineering Ltd, Portland Street, Birmingham B6 55D. Unfortunately production is now limited to metal buttons, mainly for uniform manufacturers.

CABOCHON BUTTONS

A CABOCHON is simply a polished stone of no intrinsic value, sometimes slightly cut, but with one side absolutely flat and the other allowed to retain its natural, rounded form. Many buttons today are called cabochon that are, in fact, made from moulded pieces of coloured glass. Real cabochon buttons are not easy to find.

CALICO BUTTONS

THESE are not in fact buttons made from calico but small china buttons, pierced with two or four holes for sewing, and decorated by transfer with patterns imitating calico cloth, on a white background. They were manufactured in France and in England from about the middle of the nineteenth century. Calico buttons were cheap and are not considered to be collectors' items.

CAMEO BUTTONS

A CAMEO was originally an engraved gem on which a design was worked in relief. The usual material used for a cameo was a semi-precious stone, such as onyx, cornelian, agate or sardonyx, but

Shell cameo buttons surrounded by a cut-steel border, in the style of the 1880s.

sometimes precious stones such as amethysts, emeralds and even diamonds were used. Very few buttons made from precious stones are to be found today except perhaps in museums. The *Cabinet des Medailles* of the National Library in Paris, has a set of twelve cameo buttons in sardonyx which belonged to King Henry IV (1553–1610), but such items arc rarc. Button collectors now recognise two kinds of cameo buttons, those made out of stone and those made out of mother-of-pearl or shell. Shell cameos are commonly carved from the Cassis Rufa, from the East Indian seas, the Cassis Cornuta, found near Madagascar, and the Cassis Tuberca from the West Indies. They are now very valuable finds. Some buttons, mostly made of glass and also moulded rather than carved, were made to imitate the genuine cameos.

Shell cameo buttons made in the nineteenth century are still to be found in the form of one-piece buttons, or mounted on metal frames, sometimes with a border of paste brilliants or cut steel.

CELLINI, BENVENUTO

CELLINI was a Florentine sculptor and goldsmith (1500–1571), pupil of Michelangelo. In about 1530, he made an extraordinary button for Pope Clement VII, mounted on gold and decorated with diamonds and other precious stones, and depicting God the Father, surrounded by cherubs. The button has disappeared, but the British Museum has a representation of it in a watercolour by F. Bartoli.

29

CLOTH BUTTONS

CLOTH buttons are rarely of interest to collectors, although millions of them were made up to about 1930. Since then they have been made only on request to adorn *haute couture* dresses. All the cloth buttons or *boutons-tailleurs*, as they are called in France, were made by covering bone, ivory, wood or metal with various types of fabrics, handmade at the beginning in the eighteenth century and machine-made from the nineteenth century onwards.

COIN BUTTONS

THERE are two different types of coin buttons, one made with a real coin and the other made from the design of a real coin. The idea of manufacturing buttons from coins or to look like coins dates from at least the seventeenth century, and the popularity of the genre survives. Some are cheap stamped metal picture buttons made to resemble various kinds of coins, mostly Greek and Roman, but also Austrian, French, English, German and Dutch. Other, valuable examples are made of silver.

Button made with a real 1902 Coronation coin.

Three imitation coin buttons.

30

Coin buttons in stamped metal manufactured to look like real antique coins.

COPENHAGEN PORCELAIN

THE Royal Porcelain Factory of Copenhagen was started in 1774, by Heinrich Muller, with the help of deserters from the early German factories. During the latter part of the eighteenth century, the factory produced beautiful buttons, undecorated, of various types and sizes, in hard paste porcelain. Practically all these buttons are marked on the back with the well-known sign of the three waves, in blue under cover. Many buttons of smaller size, hand-decorated with polychrome flowers, and bearing a similar mark, can still be found, but they belong to the nineteenth century.

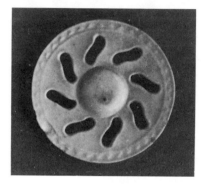

Above: Danish porcelain button of the Royal Copenhagen factory bearing the blue wave mark.

Top left, right and bottom right: 18th-century Danish porcelain buttons from the Royal Copenhagen factory, each bearing the mark of the three blue waves.

COPPER BUTTONS

COPPER has frequently been used in the manufacture of buttons, particularly in the eighteenth century when the frames of underglass buttons were usually of copper. Nineteenth-century underglass buttons are distinguished from those of the earlier period by the fact that their frames are made of brass.

A great number of copper buttons of the plainer type were produced practically everywhere in Europe during the eighteenth century. Most of them are of the one-piece, flat kind, decorated with hand-engraved or engine-turned designs. Due to their strong construction, many of them have survived and can still be found.

18th-century French copper button.

Set of five 18th-century Birmingham copper buttons. Reproduced by kind permission of Birmingham City Museums and Art Gallery.

CORAL BUTTONS

THIS type of button is very old and, as its production was very limited, it is rarely found. Old French documents mention that in the reign of Charles IX (1550–1574), son of Henry II, Parisian buttonmakers produced beautiful buttons, 'as fine as jewellery made at the time, notably in silver, niello—always hand-chased—and, more rarely, coral buttons'. It would appear, therefore, that the first coral buttons were made during the sixteenth century. Buttons made of coral are very rarely mentioned in documents, for they seem to have been made only to order. Coral has been used sometimes to decorate buttons of other types including some made for the tourist trade in the nineteenth and twentieth centuries, notably in Italy.

CORALENE BUTTONS

THESE are buttons decorated with tiny glass beads, which can be hollow or solid, coloured or plain. In the eighteenth century, pearls were sometimes used, the pearls sewn on to the button exactly matching others sewn on to the clothing itself. The French call this type *sac à perles*. Most buttons of this type were, however, made during the nineteenth century, when beads were sometimes sewn directly on to a cloth button or were stuck on to a glass background. More recently, beads forming a design, for instance of a bouquet of flowers, have been sewn to a flat metal base pierced with small holes.

CROCHET BUTTONS

CROCHET is a rustic lace made with a single hook (the crochet hook) or long needle made out of metal, bone or plastic, and crooked at one end. The art of crochet is not quite dead but our forebears made bedspreads, tablecloths, blouses and even dresses in crochet. Buttons were made in crochet at the end of the nineteenth century. Wooden or cardboard bases were simply covered with tight crochet lace. Most of those buttons have unfortunately disappeared and they are not much sought after. They were usually either black or white, pastel-coloured threads having been used sparingly. Crochet buttons in the form of a ball entirely covered with a crochet net were stuffed with cotton or cotton wool and always home-made.

Far right: French crochet buttons made in Paris in 1883 (Collection Wittamer, Brussels).

34

DAMASCENE

THIS was a technique used to decorate steel, mainly used by armourers to decorate guns and sword blades. It consists of inlaying thin silver or gold wires into grooves carved with a sharp tool into a steel plate. A few eighteenth-century steel buttons were decorated in this way.

DARNAUDERY

DARNAUDERY was the name of a celebrated French buttonmaker, supplier to the king, whose shop was in the Palais Royal in Paris, at the sign of the *Toilette d'or*, during the last quarter of the eighteenth century. A contemporary article in the magazine *Magasin des modes*, just before the taking of the Bastille, describes Darnaudery's wares as buttons decorated with 'diamond-chips' (evidently paste brilliants), jewel buttons in silver and gold, underglass buttons painted with historical scenes from the reign of King Henry IV, steel buttons from England and from France, enamel buttons with Etruscan designs, cameo buttons in the manner of Roman antiques, and Italian agate buttons. The acquisition of any of these buttons is a collector's dream.

DECOUPAGE BUTTONS

THE art of *découpage* consists of taking a chosen motif in paper and sticking it, as artistically as possible, on to its base (usually wood) and then covering it with several coats of varnish. This decorative technique was first used in Italy, then in France and Belgium during the eighteenth century to decorate pieces of furniture, boxes and mirrors. Découpage buttons were made in France during the eighteenth century. Tiny pieces of paper were stuck to a coloured background, the results being then inserted in an underglass button. This type of button is very rare.

DELFT BUTTONS

THE Dutch town of Delft was famous, in the sixteenth, seventeenth and eighteenth centuries, for its production of lead glazed earthenware. The Dutch are still producing such earthenware items, decorated in blue and white, and souvenir shops in Holland are full of them, but they have very little to do with the real old Delft, which is so eagerly collected. One can still find buttons in so-called Delft, some mounted on silver, but they are made for the tourist trade and are not collectors' items.

DICE BUTTONS

'NOVELTY' representational buttons have been common in Europe from the eighteenth century onwards, and buttons picturing miniature playing cards (see p. 94) or shaped like dice were among the many curiosities produced by the button manufacturers in France and England.

Rare set of dice buttons in black glass with the dots handpainted.

Stamped metal button of the 19th century decorated with a dice.

DORSET BUTTONS

THE Dorset button was made only in England, originally in the county of Dorset (which gave it its name) in the middle of the eighteenth century. It was hand made, very often by lacemakers, and consists simply of a ring of wire with threads drawn over and over it and gathered in the centre to form a cartwheel. The Dorset button does not attract many collectors. It was replaced in the middle of the nineteenth century by the English three-fold linen button, invented by Humphrey Jeffries of Birmingham and first marketed in 1841 by the firm of John Aston (see entry Three-fold Linen Button p. 120).

EGLOMISE BUTTONS

THIS is a very ancient technique which consisted of covering the reverse side of a piece of glass with lacquered paint, gold or silver, motifs being then cut out of the layer of gold with a very sharp tool. A second coat of black or other coloured paint was then applied to fill the details cut out of the gold. The finished glass was inserted in a small round frame. The technique of *églomisé* was revived in France by a picture-frame-maker called Glomy, whose name was thus given to the technique. Many beautiful buttons in *églomisé* glass were made in the eighteenth century.

Eglomisé French revolutionary buttons of around 1790 mounted on copper frames. Wittamer Collection, Brussels.

EGYPTIAN REVIVAL BUTTONS

BETWEEN 1800 and 1830, and again between 1860 and 1880, there was a vogue for buttons reflecting the interest in Egyptology, which followed archeological discoveries in Egypt. The first period saw the production of buttons of high quality which are now very rare, and

Picture buttons with Egyptian designs.

38

include a well known type with ornamental Egyptian designs in bronze applied to semi-precious stones. The second period saw a number of these picture buttons made of cheaper metal.

French button from a set of eight with Egyptian figures in gilt bronze applied to a background of coral. Empire period.

ELIZABETHAN DESIGNS

MANY buttons, mostly picture buttons from the second half of the nineteenth century, feature sixteenth-century scenes and figures, including a number of heads of women wearing the ruffles and lace collars typical of the Elizabethan period.

Picture buttons with Elizabethan designs. 19th century.

DAIN, WATTS, AND MANTON,

(SUCCESSORS TO WILLIAM ELLIOTT AND SONS,)

Patentees and Button Manufacturers,

Regent Works, BIRMINGHAM; and No. 38, Noble Street, Foster Lane, LONDON.

ELLIOTT, WILLIAM AND SON

A BUTTON-making firm founded in Birmingham in 1818, William Elliott's was situated in Regent Street and principally concerned with the manufacture of gilt and plated buttons for the Royal Navy and the British Army, livery buttons and metal-mounted mother-of-pearl buttons. Later, they had premises in Frederick Street. In 1837 Elliott patented a fancy silk button with a centred pattern, and, although the patent was hotly disputed and many imitations were produced elsewhere, Elliott and Son became one of the largest manufacturers in Birmingham. It is said that as many as sixty looms were at one time employed in London making the special material the factory required. William Elliott also improved upon the linen button patented by John Aston. The firm was taken over about 1850

40

by Messrs Dain, Watts and Manton, of Regent Works, Regent Street, Birmingham.

ENAMEL BUTTONS

THE art of enamelling, practiced by the jewellers of Byzantium between the seventh and twelfth centuries, had been known a long time before that by the Chinese, Indian, Roman and Persian goldsmiths, not to mention the Mycenians, practically two thousand years before Christ. It was revived in Western Europe during the eleventh century when Byzantine workers were invited first to Italy and Sicily and then further north. Schools developed near Limoges in France and along the Rhine and the Meuse. We know that the first enamel buttons were made during the sixteenth century in France, as they were worn by François I. We also know that Charles IX issued, in July 1566, regulations pertaining to the work of the Parisian 'enamellers-buttonmakers' and that subsequent regulations were issued by Henry III, in April 1583, regarding the work of all 'enamel, glass and crystal buttonmakers'. Unfortunately, all the buttons made of enamel in the sixteenth and seventeenth centuries seem to have disappeared completely and only a small number of eighteenth-century buttons are left for collectors. Most of the enamel buttons still to be found today were made during the nineteenth century when buttonmakers from France, England, Russia and Germany made and sold beautiful buttons made of enamels, opaque or translucent, colourless or multi-coloured.

French enamel Art Nouveau buttons.

41

Far left: Beautiful set of eight different English enamel buttons made in Birmingham during the second half of the 18th century. Reproduced by kind permission of Birmingham City Museums and Art Gallery.

Two sets of 18th-century Birmingham enamel buttons. Brussels Museum of Art and History.

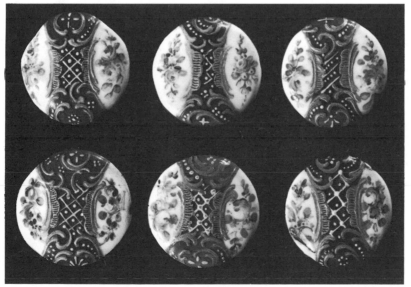

Rare French 18th-century painted enamel buttons mounted on copper frames.

Rare Russian spherical enamel button made by the *cloisonné* technique. Kostroma hallmark for 1903.

French 19th-century painted enamel button mounted on silver and surrounded by a paste border. Very rare.

Set of six English enamel buttons mounted on silver, in the original box. London hallmark for 1903.

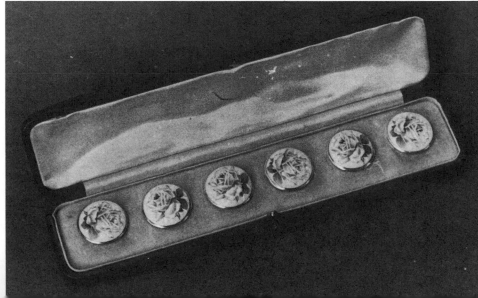

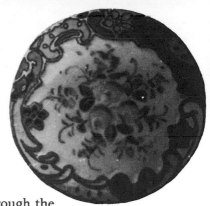

Painted enamel buttons with *champlevé* borders.

The techniques for making enamel have not changed through the centuries, and buttons of all the different types can be found. The rarest are of *cloisonné* enamel. In *cloisonné*, the enamel is poured into compartments formed by thin metal strips which have been previously soldered to the surface of the plate. In *champlevé*, a method developed mainly during the twelfth century, the enameller first carves his compartments out of the metal, and the enamel is poured into the cavities. A similar method is *basse-taille* when, by working with a chisel in very high relief, compartments of various depths are achieved and filled with translucent enamels producing varying degrees of chromatic intensity. A fourth method was *émaux peints,* or enamel painted on plaques covering the entire surface of the underlying metal. Many buttons decorated in *grisaille* belong to this category. *A jour* enamelling is a technique rarely used in buttonmaking: the very rare buttons *à jour* still extant were made like a normal *cloisonné,* but without soldering the wires to the metal base. The enamel, always translucent, was poured into the cavity-

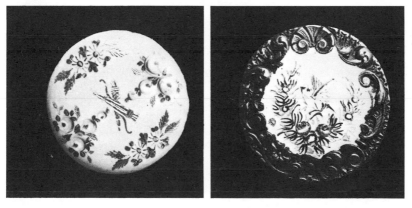

French 18th-century enamel buttons.

Very unusual large French enamel
button of the 19th century made in the
manner of the ancient Limoges
enamels.

Large *champlevé* enamel button of the
19th century, probably French.

Champlevé enamel buttons. 19th century.

compartments and the finished product looked rather like a
miniature stained-glass window. Some buttons, mainly made during
the nineteenth century, are also decorated with enamel dots,
imitating jewels, turquoise blue being the colour most frequently
reproduced.

Many motifs have appeared on enamel buttons, flowers being the most popular. Collectors look particularly for painted scenes, portrait heads, birds or animals, but some buttons decorated with geometrical designs are well worth collecting.

Rare and unusual French *champlevé* enamel button in the form of a flower with a cut steel centre. 19th century.

ETCHING

A TECHNIQUE of print-making in which the plate is not engraved or cut with a tool but eaten into (etched) by acid. Quite a number of eighteenth-century underglass buttons were decorated by inserting an etching under the glass. It is perhaps surprising that the technique never seems to have been used for decorating metal buttons.

ETTERBEEK

A HARD paste porcelain factory was founded in 1787 in Etterbeek in Belgium (now a suburb of Brussels) by a certain Chrêtien Kuhne, a German from Iserlohn in Westphalia. The factory ceased manufacture in 1803, after having produced a vast number of beautiful porcelain pieces of graceful and original design. The decoration is superb, particularly on the pieces hand-painted by Louis Cretté. All the buttons are marked on the back with the monogram E.B., for Etterbeek-Brussels.

These beautiful buttons were made by the Etterbeek porcelain factory in 1789 to commemorate the Belgian revolution that year against the Austrian army of occupation.

47

ETYMOLOGY OF THE WORD 'BUTTON'

THE exact origin of the word 'button' (*bouton* in French) is unknown, although some people think that it might have come from the old German word *botan*, which became *bouter* in French. The meaning of the French verb *bouter,* which is hardly used today as it is very archaic, is to 'push' or 'set'. This explanation is supported by the fact that in the thirteenth century the word was written *boton* in French, which is very similar to the German *botan*. Whatever the origin of the word, according to certain French sources the idea of using a button to fasten garments was made popular in western Europe by the returning Crusaders. The earliest recorded use of the written word is by the unknown author of the French *Chanson de Roland* in the twelfth century. He wrote: *'consels d'orgeul ne vaut mie un boton'* (counsels of pride are not worth a button). It must be remembered that the word 'button' originally meant any small projection.

FANCY JEWELLED BUTTONS

FANCY jewelled buttons appeared during the eighteenth century, mainly when the French buttonmakers replaced real stones with the much cheaper paste (or *strass* as it was and is still called in French). Paste rapidly became the poor man's diamond. Diamonds were most frequently imitated, but in the eighteenth century makers often used blue paste on buttons. Production continued uninterrupted throughout the nineteenth and twentieth centuries, Paris remaining the main production centre.

In the nineteenth century, buttonmakers produced buttons of all types, always highly decorated, many with moulded glass in a variety of colours. Some were made with a single glass stone in the centre, mounted on metal. Buttons of this type were used on women's coats.

FIBULA

THE fibula of ancient times and the Middle Ages, a kind of clasp to hold together two pieces of clothing on the shoulder or on the chest, is the ancestor of the button. It was replaced by the button in France between 1220 and 1270.

FILIGREE BUTTONS

FILIGREE buttons were usually made of silver wires, although gold and other metal wires have also been used. They had a spherical shape and sometimes carried a hallmark. They were made as early as the sixteenth century, but most were made during the eighteenth and nineteenth centuries in various countries of eastern Europe, in Scandinavia and, of course, in Italy, Genoa being most renowned for their production. Some collectors also include buttons decorated with stamped lace-like designs in this category.

FIRMIN AND SONS LTD

THE earliest British button factory was founded in 1670 by Thomas Firmin in Three Kings' Court, London. Since that date there has always been a Firmin firm in England, although its history is rather sketchy until 1770, when Samuel Firmin was in business, first near Somerset House, then in the Strand. The firm became Firmin and Westall, in 1797, then Philip Firmin in 1812. From 1815 until 1823, it was known as Firmin and Langdale, the name Firmin and Sons appearing for the first time in 1824. It was then known as Robert Firmin in 1826 with additional premises at Clare Court, Drury Lane, and again as Firmin and Sons in 1839, with a branch at White Horse Yard, Drury Lane. In 1841 the name was changed to Philip and Samuel Firmin. Then in 1875 the firm became a limited company. It moved from the Strand to 109 St Martin's Lane and a factory was opened in Hockley, Birmingham. In 1915, the Company moved to Cork Street and finally, in 1968, to 81 Ford Road, London. Firmin buttons are quite commonly found today and their backmarks help to date them. They are mainly military, naval and livery buttons.

FLOWERS

BUTTONS featuring all types of flowers have been produced by the

Metal buttons decorated with flowers. 19th century.

billion throughout Europe, in every conceivable material, starting in the eighteenth century when real flowers were sometimes inserted under glass. Flower decorations were used on enamel and porcelain buttons in the eighteenth, nineteenth and even twentieth centuries. Flowers are also found on countless picture buttons of the late nineteenth century, on black and coloured glass and on *passementerie* buttons of the eighteenth and nineteenth centuries. Flowers have been painted on wood and on ivory, carved in mother-of-pearl, engraved on steel and moulded in horn. Some collectors specialise in flower buttons.

19th-century metal picture buttons decorated with flowers.

FRAGONARD, JEAN-HONORE

THE famous French painter (1732–1806), pupil of Chardin and of Boucher, also painted buttons, including at least one set of underglass buttons decorated with idealised country scenes in the manner of Watteau.

50

FREEMASONRY

FREEMASONRY has not inspired the buttonmakers of France, nor often those of England and elsewhere as the Masons are a secret society and members do not wear buttons advertising their lodges. Masonic buttons are therefore very rare. But they do exist, mainly in the United States. There are also some in Britain where buttons bearing the usual Masonic ornaments have been found, usually in stamped metal, but also in enamel, in mother-of-pearl or glass, mounted in metal frames and crowned with the insignia of Freemasonry in silver or other metal.

English Masonic button of the 19th-century in gilt metal with a background of blue glass.

GALENA

GALENA (from the Greek *Galenê*, meaning lead) is a natural sulphide, of a solid metallic grey, the main ore of lead. Buttons were not made with it, but ground galena was often sprinkled on to the paper base of nineteenth-century buttons, giving them a glittering appearance.

GEDOYN, PIERRE

GEDOYN was a Parisian goldsmith and buttonmaker from whom François I ordered a set of 'eight black enamel buttons, mounted on gold, with "antique letters" applied to the enamel'. For this set, Gedoyn received twelve pounds. The record is important as it is the first mention of enamel buttons.

GILT BUTTONS

BUTTONS in solid gold have been made for hundreds of years, although mainly during the eighteenth and nineteenth centuries. They were intended both for civilian use and to adorn officers' uniforms. Most of these seem to have disappeared completely and they are rarely found nowadays. More easily found today are machine-made gilt buttons, usually made of brass and covered with a very thin coat of gold. This type of button was first manufactured around 1790 by the Birmingham buttonmakers and continued to be

51

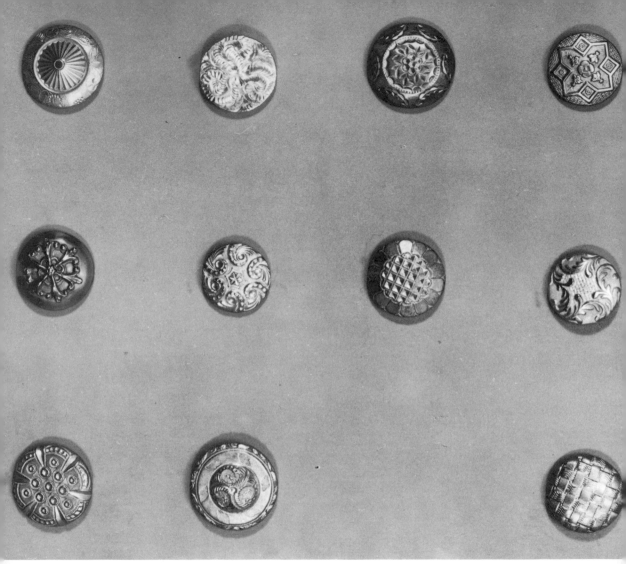

Early 19th-century English gilt buttons. All carry marks such as 'Rich orange', 'Treble gilt', 'Extra Gilt' or 'Superfine quality'.

made until the middle of the nineteenth century. Until about 1820, gilt buttons were of one-piece design, always flat, sparsely decorated and fitted with an Alpha shank. As they were not striking enough at first sight to attract the attention of potential customers, indications such as 'Rich Colour', 'Treble Gilt', 'Rich Orange Colour Gilt', and

'Extra Rich' started to be stamped upon the reverse side. Around 1830, gilt buttons were greatly improved and became artistically much more attractive although they were still machine-made. they were now decorated with fancy motifs in high relief, sometimes worked by hand. These later buttons, of the two-piece design, were fitted with an Omega shank. Later, around 1850, they were fitted with a Sanders-type shank. The French buttonmakers made the same type of buttons, but they are frankly inferior in quality to the English models. Perhaps the most attractive of these 'golden age' buttons are the 'watchcase type', so called because the top of the button resembles a real gold watchcase, always finely engraved.

English 19th-century gilt buttons.

GLASS BUTTONS

GLASS buttons have been made for a very long time and it is recorded that Philip the Good, Duke of Burgundy, ordered some Venetian glass buttons (*ouvrages de Venise*) decorated with pearls.

Rare 19th-century paperweight-style glass button.

19th-century French milk glass button handpainted with gold.

Black glass button of about 1880, decorated with cut steel facets and crescents.

53

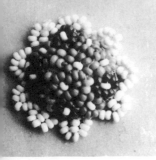

Unusual glass button, of the type called *'sac a perles'* by the French, made up of a number of tiny glass beads.

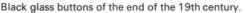

Black glass buttons of the end of the 19th century.

Handpainted black glass button mounted on metal frame.

Glass buttons were made in England at least from the end of the seventeenth century. The *London Gazette* of 17 March 1687 makes mention of 'one coat with black glass buttons'. There are also references to glass buttons in English documents between 1687 and 1766, and the *Birmingham Directory* for 1770 mentions the existence in that city of 'glass pinchers', or artists preparing the glass reserved for the making of link-buttons. Billions of these buttons were made in Europe and the greatest period of their manufacture began about 1840. They were made in England, France, Italy, Germany and particularly Czechoslovakia.

Left: 19th-century white glass button with a gilt escutcheon decorated with paste. Centre, right: 19th-century black glass buttons.

19th-century glass buttons decorated with heads of women, one in base metal, the other in solid silver.

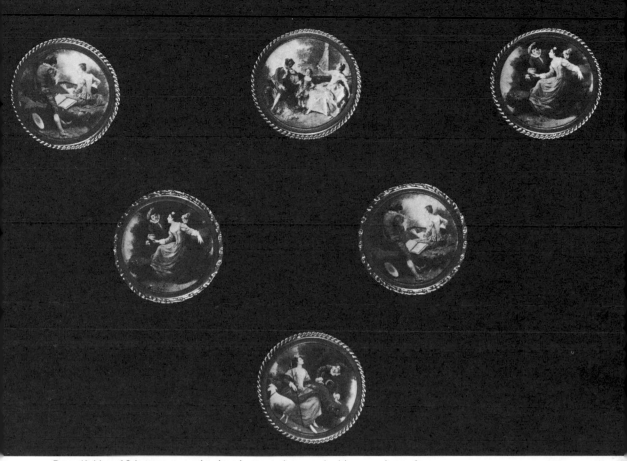

Beautiful late 19th-century underglass buttons decorated with engravings of scenes *à la* Watteau. During the 18th century this type of button was usually mounted on copper, but these are mounted on gilt frames.

There were many types and many colours. Collectors today put their finds into two main categories, black and coloured glass. The most sought after of the black glass buttons are those decorated with idyllic scenes, flowers, human heads, interior scenes and landscapes, together with those which feature imitation cameo-heads and various designs in imitation intaglio. Some black glass buttons are inlaid with silver, fragments of coloured glass or shells. Others are painted under the glass; others enamelled in the manner of Mary Gregory glass; still others painted with lustre paint. Under the heading of coloured glass there are many different types: frosted glass, crackled glass, some with metal designs embedded in it, some

Black glass button decorated with flower and butterfly in reverse.

55

inlaid with other materials, some designed in moulded glass to look like lace and others with an outline design moulded into the glass and filled with paint. Among the most attractive are paperweight buttons and those where the glass simply covers a drawing made on paper, the whole resembling a miniature paperweight. Some very rare buttons, which are often spherical in form, are made of blown glass. Others, produced between the two World Wars, are shaped to resemble many objects, including heads, hearts, animals and vegetables (see Realistics p. 101).

19th-century black glass button mounted on metal frame and decorated with an inlaid butterfly of coloured glass.

Different types of black glass buttons. 19th century.

There would be no end to a collection of glass buttons, which were popular up to the time of the Second World War, when they started being replaced by plastic buttons. It would pay collectors to concentrate on specific types.

Moulded glass button mounted on metal frame.

Beautiful French glass button made about 1900.

Small paperweight button manufactured in Bohemia. 19th century.

56

GOLF CLUB BUTTONS

GOLF clubs, mainly in Great Britain, issued specially made buttons for their members as early as the nineteenth century. Most are in gilt or silvered metal and they are always stamped. These are not easy to find however, and are of little interest to collectors, except to those who are keen on golf. They feature golf players or crossed golf clubs and bear the name of the particular club.

GOSDEN, THOMAS

GOSDEN was a London buttonmaker, known today by collectors for his one-piece, engraved sporting and hunting buttons which he manufactured as early as 1820. These very beautiful buttons were usually manufactured in sets of sixteen. Each button carries an inscription, originally 'Sold only by T. Gosden, 16 Bedford Street, Covent garden'. Later, the inscription was changed to 'Sold only by T. Gosden, Charing Cross, London, 107 St Martin's Lane'.

GOTHIC REVIVAL

ABOUT 1840, at the height of the Romantic Period, there was a revival of interest in the Gothic style, both in France and in England, and the buttonmakers of both countries started manufacturing beautiful buttons, mostly in metal, featuring Gothic-type decorations such as heads of knights, St George and the Dragon, pieces of armour, or depictions of chivalric adventures. These buttons, some quite large, were usually round, but some are square and all date from the middle of the nineteenth century. They should not be confused with some modern buttons of poor quality which also feature pseudo-Gothic designs. The old buttons were heavy while the modern ones are much lighter.

GRANCHEZ

A FRENCH buttonmaker active in Paris during the second half of the eighteenth century, Granchez had premises at the sign of *'Le Petit Dunkerque'* at the corner of the Quai Conti and the Rue Dauphine.

According to French documents, in his shop were to be found, among other items, some of the most beautiful buttons of the Louis XVI period. The magazine *Cabinet des Modes* in its issue dated 1 January 1786 reveals that Granchez had in his stock steel engraved buttons and others, in the shape of a pyramid, decorated with Hebrew hieroglyphics.

GRANITE BUTTONS

GRANITE buttons are very rare indeed. We know only that they were being manufactured in Scotland towards the middle of the nineteenth century, with granite from Aberdeen and Peterhead, by the firm of George Jameson of Aberdeen.

GREEN, CADBURY AND RICHARDS

THIS was a very important firm of buttonmakers founded in Birmingham in the 1860s. Their first factory, the Friday Bridge Works, was in Summer Row, and in 1876, the firm moved to a brand new factory, the Great Hampton Street Works, where it employed as many as 400 workers. The same year, the firm bought Pearl Button Business of Clement Street, Birmingham, following the death of its owner, S. A. Rowley. Right from the start, this Birmingham firm produced enormous numbers of buttons of all types (between 120,000 and 200,000 per week). The firm's speciality was a linen button known as 'The very button', plain and two-holed, familiar before the First World War to every woman in Great Britain and also known throughout the world. This type of utilitarian button is not, of course, collected today, but the firm produced millions of other buttons of excellent workmanship: 'a large variety of linen buttons from the best Belfast linen, tailor's buttons, pearl, gilt and plated livery buttons, crest buttons, naval and military buttons, mother-of-pearl, enamel, ivory, silver and gold, paste buttons of all shapes and sizes'.

The firm no longer exists, but its splendid factory in Great Hampton Street still stands and is now occupied by a firm of wholesale ring merchants.

Green, Cadbury & Co., in Great Hampton St.

WORKS, BIRMINGHAM.

GREENAWAY, KATE

THE celebrated illustrations for children's books of the English writer and artist Kate Greenaway (1846–1901) were often reproduced on button faces at the end of the nineteenth century. Certain Kate Greenaway buttons have also been reproduced in the United States.

GREUZE, JEAN-BAPTISTE

THIS distinguished eighteenth-century French painter (1725–1805) painted idyllic country scenes on enamel buttons produced in Paris, in the manner of Fragonard.

GRISAILLE

GRISAILLE is a method of painting in grey monochrome to give the illusion of relief. It was first used by European enamellers during the early sixteenth century. The method was most often used in the eighteenth century, for painting on enamels, on porcelain and ivory. Buttons decorated in this style can still be found, mostly made of enamel.

GUILLAUMOT

GUILLAUMOT is a French firm specialising in heraldic engravings, founded in 1761 in the Galérie de Montpensier, in the Palais Royal, Paris, by a certain Decourcelle. He was succeeded by Desmarets, Bessaignet and then Simon. This very ancient firm is still in business in Paris where for more than two hundred years it has produced thousands of livery and hunting buttons in silver and other metals.

GUILLOCHE

GUILLOCHE is a decorative technique used mainly by jewellers. It consists of engraving, with a sharp tool or in a lathe, parallel wavy lines on a metallic surface to form a base pattern, sometimes most attractively covered with transparent enamel. This type of decoration is found on many nineteenth-century buttons.

HALLMARKS

NEARLY all over the world, objects made from precious metals should be stamped with a guarantee mark: gold and silver buttons should therefore carry such a stamp. But this is not always the case except in Great Britain, Holland, Norway and, to a certain extent, Russia. In France, compulsory hallmarking of silver and gold buttons ceased officially in 1822. It is therefore usually easy to identify and date buttons made in Great Britain, but more difficult to do the same for those made elsewhere. Even if the hallmarks are present, it sometimes takes a specialist to decipher them.

HAMMOND, TURNER AND SONS LTD

IN its time if not the biggest, at least one of the oldest button factories in the world, this company is reputed to have been founded in

Birmingham in 1717. The firm occupied premises at what is known as Number 100 Snowhill until the turn of the last century, when it moved to Summer Hill and the Goodman Street Button Works. In the middle of the nineteenth century the firm was noted for its metal buttons, particularly uniform buttons. In the 1903 directories Hammond, Turner and Sons are described as 'manufacturers of ivory, horn, glass, metal, linen, naval, military and other gilt buttons, also studs, solitaires and links, ladies clasps, etc.'. The firm disappeared from the Birmingham directories *circa* 1955.

HARRISON AND SMITH LTD

BUTTONS with the reverse side stamped with this name are sometimes found, but nothing much is known about the firm which produced them. James Harrison, of Alma Street, Birmingham, appears for the first time in the local directories in 1875. By the turn of the century, Harrison and Smith were describing themselves as 'general button and military ornament manufacturers'.

HEATON, RALPH

HEATON was an English buttonmaker whose business premises were in Sloane Street, Birmingham, at the end of the eighteenth century. His production is not well known, except that for the most part he produced shanks for the other buttonmakers of the city.

HIGHLAND DRESS BUTTONS

TRADITIONAL Highland dress is always decorated with beautifully designed buttons made in silver or white metal. These buttons, which are worn on all Highland dress, military as well as civilian, are rather small, square or diamond-shaped or, very occasionally, round. The stamped designs represent Scotsmen, thistles, or the Scottish lion rampant surrounded by mottos in Gaelic. This type of button, which dates from the nineteenth century, is still worn in Scotland and is therefore still being manufactured, making it difficult for collectors to tell the new from the old unless, of course, they are in hallmarked silver.

Silver-plated Highland dress buttons of the usual diamond shape.

HISTORICAL BUTTONS

HISTORICAL events have inspired buttonmakers ever since the eighteenth century, although the buttons were not always manufactured at the time of the event, but very often much later. Certain collectors tend to include in this category armed forces buttons, commemorative buttons and the like, but historical buttons should strictly depict actual events, such as the landing of Christopher Columbus, Admiral Peary reaching the North Pole, the first balloon ascents, the landing on the moon, or the inauguration of the Eiffel Tower. These buttons, which are certainly worth collecting, are unfortunately not very common.

HORN BUTTONS

19th-century pressed horn button.

FROM the eighteenth century onwards, an enormous number of natural and moulded horn buttons were manufactured in Europe, particularly in France and Germany. There are two different categories of horn, the 'head horn', from the antlers or horns of various animals, and the 'foot horn', from the hooves of horses and cows. The first type of button was made by slicing antlers by hand or by machine, the resulting horn discs then being made into buttons. This type was manufactured particularly in Bavaria and Austria during the nineteenth century and was known in France as the 'buffalo button'.

French 19th-century horn hunting buttons.

'Foot horn buttons' were made by cutting the hoof in two parts, which were then flattened by machines. Small discs were cut out of the pieces, heated to a high temperature, placed in moulds and pressed. At this stage of manufacture other materials, such as mother-of-pearl, silver and other metals were added for decorative purposes. Most of the moulded horn buttons to be found today were machine-made during the nineteenth century and the first buttons of this type were made in Birmingham in the early 1800s. They are quite common, and most are decorated with the heads of various animals in high relief. Sometimes they are left in their natural colour but many have been chemically dyed black or blue.

Notable horn buttonmakers were T. W. Ingram and Thomas Cox in Birmingham, and Thomas Harris in Halesowen, but the best buttons of this type were made in France, notably by Emile Bassot. It was Bassot who first had the idea of embedding a wire shank in his horn buttons. His invention was quickly adopted in England.

HUNTING BUTTONS

FIRST made in the eighteenth century to decorate the costumes of hunters and game-keepers, most hunting buttons were of very beautiful design, in silver, brass, natural or moulded horn, and sometimes in mother-of-pearl. They were very often illustrated with hunting scenes, with heads of various animals, or with animal

Set of three solid silver hunting buttons, possibly Polish. 19th century.

Left: French hunting buttons of the middle of the 19th century.
Above: English hunting buttons of the first half of the 19th century.

figures shown in their natural surroundings. Most commonly represented were dogs of different breeds, horses, deer, boar, foxes, wolves, eagles, partridges and pheasants. The most sought-after buttons of this type are the English silver and French enamel buttons of the eighteenth century, which are both rare. Hunting buttons made in the manner of the picture buttons, in stamped brass or metal, were widely used during the nineteenth century all over the world. The English gilt buttons of the first part of the nineteenth century are probably among the most attractive.

English brass hunting buttons. 19th century.

Above: Rare set of eight French hunting buttons in brass from the first half of the 19th century.

Above: Enlarged versions of two of the above buttons.

English 18th-century carved mother-of-pearl hunting button.

HUNTING CLUBS

THERE have for two centuries been hunting clubs or 'Hunts', as they are known in England, throughout Europe and particularly in England and France. And club members often wore distinctive buttons made of gold, silver or other metal. In England these were almost always decorated with a fox's head, a running fox or a riding-whip, together with the club initials. In France, where actual clubs with members, in the English style, did not exist, groups of landed gentry wore distinctive buttons. The French buttons had animal designs, depicting rabbits, deer, boar, sometimes a horse and rider, together with a hunting emblem or motto.

Stamped metal button of the 19th century showing an inanimate object, in this case a lock and a key.

'INANIMATE' BUTTONS

SO called because they were decorated with inanimate objects such as keys, locks, umbrellas, horseshoes, fans, and buckles, 'inanimate' buttons belong mostly to the picture-button category and date from the second half of the nineteenth century and the beginning of the twentieth.

INCROYABLES ET MERVEILLEUSES

IN the years following 1789, the beginning of the French Revolution, some Parisians adopted incredible and rather ridiculous fashions in order to create a stir. The men, *les incroyables*, wore trousers tight

Two 19th-century French buttons showing the well known 18th-century figures of the *Incroyables et Merveilleuses*.

just under the knees, *'à la hussarde',* very high collars and absurd hats. They always carried spiral walking sticks. The women, *'les merveilleuses',* went as far as using only transparent materials which they sometimes kept wet to make them cling to the body. Buttons on which the *Incroyables et Merveilleuses* are represented were produced in the eighteenth century, and French buttonmakers produced them well into the nineteenth century.

INLAY

INLAY is a technique of setting decorative pieces of a precious material into a base made from another (often quite common) material. Many buttons of different types have been decorated in this way, for example, silver inlaid into pearl, ivory, wood, horn or even papier mâché; pearl inlaid into papier mâché; or gold and silver into other metals.

INSECTS

NUMEROUS insects are represented on European buttons of both the eighteenth and the nineteenth centuries. Some collectors specialise in them exclusively. In the eighteenth century, insects were painted on ivory underglass or by the *eglomisé* method. Real insects were put under the domed glass of the Buffon buttons and very realistic flies were painted on waistcoat buttons of the beginning of the nineteenth century. Insects appeared again on the picture buttons of the nineteenth century and there are representations of insects encrusted in jade, mother-of-pearl, coral, ivory and wood. Bees, flies and ladybirds were the buttonmakers' favourites.

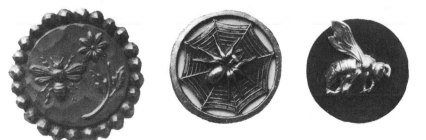

Insect buttons.

67

INTAGLIO

AN intaglio was originally an engraved gem with the design cut into it. It is the reverse of the cameo, which is cut in relief. The intaglio technique was invented by the ancient Greeks and taken up by the Romans, then, forgotten for many centuries, it was revived in Europe during the Renaissance. Real stones have sometimes been used to make buttons, but 'intaglio buttons' today are mostly moulded in various materials. Many black glass buttons are in intaglio style.

ISABEY, JEAN-BAPTISTE

IT is recorded that this well known French miniaturist, pupil of David (1767–1855), painted buttons for a living at the beginning of his career. The following extract appears in his *Memoires*: 'As it was still the fashion at the time to wear buttons as big as five franc pieces, decorated with hand-painted cherubs, flowers, country scenes, I started painting them. I got twelve "sols" for each subject.' These buttons would be very valuable today, if they could be found and authenticated.

IVORY BUTTONS

IVORY buttons have been made in Europe for a very long time. Documents show that the rosarymakers of Paris, at the beginning of the Middle Ages, were also making ivory buttons, although none seem to have survived. All kinds of lovely miniatures have been painted on ivory and inserted in buttons, and scenes have been carved out of ivory, mostly in antique design, and placed in eighteenth-century underglass buttons. Buttons can be found today in ivory inlaid with horn, mother-of-pearl and various metals. These were all manufactured, very sporadically, during the nineteenth century.

JADE BUTTONS

JADE got its name from the Spaniards who were the first Europeans to bring it back from South America, and called it *piedra de jada*. The French called it *éjade,* then *jade.* Beautiful one-piece buttons and some very rare ones mounted on metal have been found, but all of them have an Oriental or Chinese look and date from the nineteenth century. It would appear that Europeans have never used jade to make buttons.

JET BUTTONS

JET is a bituminous substance, hard and shiny black, which can be found in France in the regions of Aude, Bouches du Rhône and the Pyrenees, in Prussia, Saxony, Spain and in England. The fashion for wearing jet buttons was started by Queen Victoria when she was in mourning for her husband, Prince Albert. Of course the Queen's buttons were made with real jet from the region of Whitby, but, as they were expensive to make, copies looking exactly like jet were made of black glass. Billions of them were made during the second half of the nineteenth century and these are still to be found in grandmother's button box today. Most of the very rare real jet buttons are now in prize collections or in museums.

JEWEL BUTTONS

JEWEL buttons, made in precious metals and decorated with precious stones and pearls, are rarely found today. They were made

Jewelled buttons.

in France and England during the fourteenth century, and were popular until the end of the eighteenth century and the fall of the old régime in France. Few have been made since the French Revolution, though some examples dating from the nineteenth century have been found. It is known that two British firms, Neal and Tonks of Birmingham, and Philips Brothers of London, were making buttons in precious metals decorated with real gems around the middle of the nineteenth century.

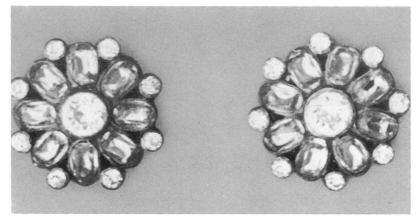

Jewelled buttons with green and white paste mounted on silver.

LAVA BUTTONS

THE lava layers from Vesuvius were a very handy source of material for the Italians, who carved the lava instead of gems to make cameos. Most represented antique heads in the manner of the ancient Greek and Roman cameos. Some were mounted on silver frames as buttons, but these are quite hard to find nowadays.

19th-century Italian lava buttons mounted on silver.

70

LIÈGE EARTHENWARE BUTTONS

THE Liège factory of Coronmeuse was founded in 1767 by a Frenchman, Nicolas Gauron, in partnership with a certain François Lefébure. It was succeeded in 1772 by another factory located on Quai Leonard, under Boussemart from Lille. The factory ceased activity in 1811. Beautiful earthenware tin-glazed buttons were made, entirely hand painted, some simply decorated with stripes of various colours, others with bouquets of flowers surrounded by garlands of roses.

Very rare set of four 18th-century Liège factory buttons in fine faience. Only thirty buttons are known to exist. Brussels Museum of Arts & History.

LITHOGRAPH BUTTONS

LITHOGRAPHY is a printing process involving drawings traced on calcareous stones with grease crayon or other medium. The process itself was invented by J. A. Senefelder of Munich in 1796, but lithograph buttons date between about 1890 and 1910. They are in fact attractive imitations of the famous eighteenth-century under-glass buttons. They are mounted on metal frames, the lithograph being placed sometimes under glass, but more often under a sheet of celluloid. Some of the most attractive are bordered in paste or in cut-steel facets. Usually lithograph buttons feature the human head, scenes being very rare indeed.

Set of four 19th-century buttons, lithographs under celluloid. One is surrounded by a border of paste.

LIVERPOOL TRANSFERS

TRANSFER-decorating was started by John Sadler of Liverpool around 1750. Soon afterwards he went into partnership with another Liverpool printer, Guy Green, to form the 'Printed Ware Manufacture'. It is not known whether Sadler produced buttons in the eighteenth century, but in the second half of the nineteenth century, buttons in porcelain, decorated with transfers, appeared on the market and those beautiful buttons are often called Liverpool transfers by collectors. This is, however, an error, since there is no evidence that they were made in Liverpool. Most of these buttons are decorated with classical heads, or, very rarely, with flowers and

72

birds. The transfers are usually in black or sepia, but polychrome designs have also been found. They are always mounted on metal and some of them show brush marks indicating that the transfers have occasionally been retouched by hand. No one has been able to discover where the porcelain discs were decorated: most of them carry no backmarks although some are marked simply 'Paris'. It is impossible even to be sure of their nationality, or whether they were in fact produced in France as well as in England.

Some buttons are mounted on heavy brass, some on very thin tin backs—a fact which might indicate the activities of two different factories. Liverpool transfers are not easy to find today.

LIVERY BUTTONS

THE first livery buttons—buttons worn by servants of noble or rich families and bearing their coats of arms—appeared throughout Europe towards the middle of the eighteenth century, mostly in France, Austria, Prussia, Belgium and England. Most livery buttons

of continental origin carry the complete coat of arms of the family, sometimes with two crests, those of both husband and wife. English livery buttons often carry only one ornament taken from the family

Set of 19th-century livery buttons depicting the coats of arms of various European noble families.

crest or, in the case of many rich but not noble English families, simply chosen according to fancy. Livery buttons not made for noble families might more properly be dubbed heraldic design buttons. Most eighteenth-century livery buttons were made as one-piece buttons in silver, and sometimes in gold. Collectors should bear in mind that a heraldic design does not make a livery button; and beware of some military buttons bearing what looks like a family coat-of-arms. Nineteenth-century livery buttons were mostly two-piece and made in brass.

19th-century livery buttons.

LUCKCOCK, JAMES

BUTTONMAKER and collector, born in 1761 and educated at the Windsor Green Academy and in Paris, Luckcock started his active life as head of the jewellery department of Samuel Pemberton's factory in Birmingham. In 1787 he started on his own as buttonmaker, with premises in St Paul's Square. He died in 1835. His own beautiful collection of about 500 eighteenth-century Birmingham buttons was given in 1943 to the Birmingham Museum of Arts and Sciences by a certain Mrs Wallis, who had inherited it. The Luckcock collection is rich in all types of rare and beautiful buttons, including hunting buttons in horn from the Cox and Ingram factory, delicate mother-of-pearl buttons, Wedgwood, jasperware, enamel and glass buttons.

MARCASITE BUTTONS

MARCASITE is an iron pyrite, faceted in the manner of precious stones. It was used to make inexpensive jewellery and buttons from the middle of the nineteenth century. At first sight marcasite buttons look like cut steel, but they can be distinguished by the fact that marcasite is never riveted from the back like cut-steel facets. Marcasite buttons have become extremely rare.

MERU

THIS small town in the department of Seine-et-Oise became the main French centre for the production of mother-of-pearl and shell buttons from about 1830. At first the making of buttons was considered to be a cottage industry and the shells were cut by hand, until 1847 when the first machine-tool became available. The buttons continued to be made at home until 1880, when the corozo nut began to be used to make buttons. The button industry had died out in Meru by the beginning of the Second World War.

MEISSEN PORCELAIN BUTTONS

THE Meissen porcelain factory in Saxony, founded in 1709 as the first European establishment of its type, is still in existence. Since 1725 the products of Meissen, erroneously called Dresden in England and Saxe in France, have been marked with two crossed swords in blue under cover. This mark was widely imitated by various factories in France, England, Belgium and Germany in the eighteenth and nineteenth centuries, and the occasional buttons decorated with polychrome flowers similar to the Meissen *deutsche blümen* and marked with the crossed swords are of doubtful origin— there is no proof that they were produced in Meissen.

MILITARY BUTTONS

STARTING a collection of military buttons is a forbidding task, since while billions of them have been manufactured throughout the world, they are very difficult to identify. Records are few, and scattered. Little, for example, is known about the buttons used by the French Army before 1784 except that they were of pewter and bore the coats of arms of various nobles. It was only at the end of the eighteenth century, under the Convention, that a regulation button was issued. It is a Chinese puzzle to find one's way through all the numbers, the eagles and the cocks which have been used at one time and another. It is also difficult to find one's way through the British military buttons, at least until 1855 when the first regulation brass buttons appeared. It should also be borne in mind that nearly every country in the world has had military buttons for centuries. With patience and determination, however, the collection of military buttons can be a rewarding hobby. A very interesting collection of ancient French buttons can be seen in the *Musée des Invalides* in Paris.

MINIATURES

BUTTONS decorated with miniatures, either hand-painted on ivory, engraved or drawn, are not among the rarest but they are the most sought after by collectors. The fashion for this type of button started in France around 1775 when a method for printing in colour was invented. The Parisian buttonmakers of the last quarter of the eighteenth century produced a vast number of *Boutons à miniature* which were always sold in sets of twelve, sixteen or twenty-four and featured such subjects as views from the voyage to Pompeii, the great Revolutionary leaders, the monuments of Paris, sets advertising hair-dressing styles, idyllic country scenes *à la* Watteau, and insects.

They are normally mounted on copper frames and covered with glass, flat or slightly domed. Such buttons were made regularly until the early nineteenth century, and the French continued occasionally to produce them to order throughout the 1880s.

MONTARSY, PIERRE LE TISSIER DE

MONTARSY was a Parisian goldsmith active at the end of the seventeenth century and main supplier of buttons to Louis XIV. The book of the king's gems and presents contains an entry, dated 3 February 1685, stating that the king paid the sum of 138,030 *livres* to Montarsy, of the *Galérie du Louvre*, for delivery of twenty-four diamond buttons. A few days later, Montarsy delivered to the Marquess of Seigneuly, 'for the king', seventy diamond buttons for which he was paid the unbelievable sum of 586,703 *livres*. That same

Above:
Set of five 19th-century underglass buttons mounted on gilt frames. The miniatures are all handpainted on ivory.

77

day, Montarsy delivered to the Palace of Versailles a set of forty-eight buttons, each composed of a single diamond mounted in gold, and sixteen other sets, of which forty-eight buttons had five diamonds each and forty-eight others had solitaire diamonds. For these the king paid 185,123 *livres*.

MOSAIC BUTTONS

THESE appeared towards the middle of the nineteenth century and were made of tiny pieces of glass or stone (tessarae) on a black background of coloured glass. Pictures of architectural ruins or buildings were most commonly shown and sometimes flowers and animals. They were made mainly in Italy, though some were made in France and others in China. The centres of these beautiful buttons were flat and highly polished in the nineteenth century, usually unpolished in the twentieth century. They were rather fragile and are rarely found in perfect condition nowadays.

Beautiful Italian Mosaic button of the middle of the 19th century.

MOTHER-OF-PEARL AND SHELL BUTTONS

MOTHER-OF-PEARL buttons, made from white deep-sea shells imported from Australia, the Philippines and Indonesia, were made in France and in England during the eighteenth century. Black mother-of-pearl buttons, from shells imported from Gambia, the Touamotu and the Fiji Islands through the ports of London and Le

Havre, were made at a later date. The white mother-of-pearl production gradually slowed down and buttonmakers, around the middle of the nineteenth century, started importing other shells such as the 'lingas' from Ceylon and Venezuela, and the 'trocas' from

Late 18th-century carved pearl buttons decorated with paste. Wittamer Collection, Brussels.

Rare 18th-century mother-of-pearl button decorated with a paste centre.

19th-century sew-through carved shell buttons.

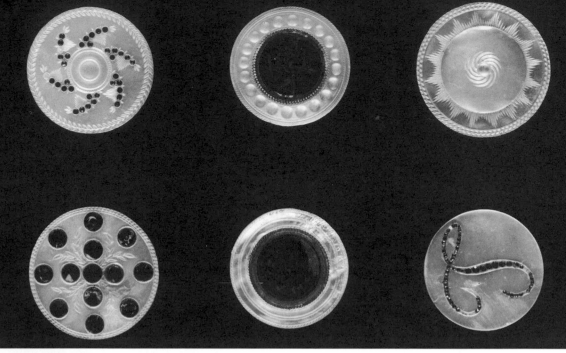

Set of six English carved pearl buttons made in Birmingham during the second half of the 18th century. Some are decorated with paste in various colours. Reproduced by kind permission of Birmingham City Museums and Art Gallery.

Japan and New Caledonia. Imports became very important. England alone imported 1800 tons in 1859, 1200 in 1860, 1100 in 1861, three quarters of them going to Birmingham. Collectors pay less attention to the origins of the shells made into buttons than to the beauty and design of the finished product. Mother-of-pearl buttons made during the eighteenth century either in Paris or Birmingham are not as rare as is supposed. Some are carved with cameo heads, some

French carved shell button of very fine workmanship mounted on metal. 19th century.

19th-century shell buttons mounted on metal frames.

Beautiful shell button decorated with a sprig of holly in solid silver.

Mother-of-pearl and shell buttons.

Mother-of-pearl
button of unusual
shape decorated with
handpainted flowers.

engraved, some both engraved and decorated with paste, but they are rarely mounted on metal frames. On the other hand, in the nineteenth century, most shell buttons were mounted on metal frames, some with paste borders, some with metal escutcheons, and many with cut steel borders. The two main European producing centres have always been Birmingham (see p. 15) and Meru (see p. 76). Undecorated pearl buttons have no value.

MYTHOLOGY

MYTHOLOGY was a source of inspiration to many buttonmakers in the eighteenth and nineteenth centuries. Scenes from antiquity are found on many eighteenth-century underglass buttons, on practically all the Wedgwood jasperware buttons mounted by Boulton of Birmingham, and on hundreds of nineteenth-century picture buttons made in cheap metal. A collection of this type of button could be assembled quite easily, but it is difficult to identify all the scenes and figures represented.

NEAL AND TONKS

BUTTONS bearing the backmarks of this firm can still occasionally be found. Unfortunately the history of the company is rather obscure. It was founded in Birmingham around the year 1855 and ceased activity in 1875. The firm's premises were at 13 Great Charles Street, Birmingham and there were produced jewel buttons and enamels, which are now very rare.

81

NIELLO

NIELLO, an Italian word from the Latin *nigellus,* meaning blackish, is a method of decorating a sheet of silver by filling engraved lines with a black composition composed of thirty-eight parts of silver, seventy-two of copper, fifty of lead and 384 of sulphur. This method was used from the Middle Ages up to the nineteenth century, when Niello buttons were still being made, but they are very rare.

The first Niello buttons known were made in France at the beginning of the sixteenth century.

NON-MILITARY UNIFORM BUTTONS

THIS heading covers the billions of buttons which were manufactured during the nineteenth and twentieth centuries, and are still being used by various organisations, government departments, towns, railways, fire brigades and so on. They can be a highly specialised form of collecting if concentrated on one single town, one province or one type of organisation, for example, railway buttons or post office buttons.

OPALINE BUTTONS

OPALINE is a word coined by modern French collectors to describe the fine coloured glass, semi-opaque and with a milky look, made during the Empire and the Restoration periods to imitate the opal-glass made in very ancient times. The secret of its production was rediscovered by the Venetian glassmakers during the sixteenth century. French glassmakers made beautiful pieces of opaline at the beginning of the nineteenth century, and those of the best period (1810–1835) were always blown. Many opaline buttons have been made, always moulded, generally white, the most attractive decorated in moulded coloured relief and painted with various motifs. Transfers have also been used to decorate them.

ORIENTAL DESIGNS

AROUND 1880, Europeans, particularly the French and English,

Various buttons of Japanese design.

'discovered' Japanese art. Painters, cabinetmakers, writers and other artists found their inspiration in the Far East. Picture buttons were in fashion at the time, and buttonmakers were quick to adopt

Set of picture buttons of Japanese inspiration. The central button is brass on a black metal background surrounded by beads in boxwood. 1880–1890.

the new fashion, producing metal buttons featuring Oriental subjects. Madame Butterfly has smiled on many buttons. Japanese warriors, musicians, strange Buddha-like figures, lovely ladies under sunshades or playing with enamel fans appeared on buttons between 1880 and the beginning of the twentieth century.

PAPIER MÂCHÉ BUTTONS

THE idea of making objects out of papier-mâché seems to have developed in France at the beginning of the eighteenth century, and the technique was perfected and commercialised in England during the second half of the century. The first to use the process was a certain Mr Watson, in his workshop at 76 High Street, Birmingham. He was followed by Henry Clay of that city, who took out a patent in 1772. It is probable that Clay was the first to make buttons in papier-mâché, but it is impossible to establish who first perfected the process of inlaying mother-of-pearl in papier-mâché. It is known that Jennens and Betteridge took over the old firm of Clay in 1816 and that they took out a patent for the inlaying of mother-of-pearl in 1825. Other unidentified firms have also produced buttons of this type. The industry faded out in England around 1865. The first French manufacturer of this type of button was J. Plaçon, who exhibited beautiful papier-mâché buttons at the Paris Exhibition of 1855. They were painted on a lacquer background and inlaid with silver and mother-of-pearl. It is also of interest that the making of papier-mâché buttons decorated with various Scottish tartans was very fashionable in Birmingham around 1852.

PARENT

THIS famous French firm of buttonmakers was founded in Paris in 1825. The firm achieved a world-wide reputation from 1886, when it was taken over by Albert Parent, whose initials A.P. appear on many buttons of great quality. It was he who invented the mark of the beehive that was stamped on most of his buttons. A few years later, Albert Parent took his brother-in-law, one Bouchard, as his partner. Their partnership continued until the end of the First World War,

84

when Albert retired leaving the firm to his son, Robert Parent, who was joined in 1924 by his brother-in-law, Balazer. The factory closed down in 1939, the two owners being called up by the French Army. Albert Parent died in 1942, but the firm was started again in 1946, its buttons being produced, however, by outside craftsmen. The firm still exists under the name Ets Parent et Corona, at 5 & 7 Rue Moret, 75011 Paris. After the Second World War, an American firm of importers, Bailey, Green and Elger, from New York, bought the collection of A.P. buttons which had been assembled by Albert Parent himself. It is known now in the United States as the 'La Ruche Collection', ('*ruche*' means beehive in French), but the 'Parent collection' would seem more appropriate.

PARISIAN BUTTONMAKERS OF THE LOUIS XVI AND EMPIRE PERIOD

TO help collectors and historians, set out below is a list of known Parisian buttonmakers active at the end of the eighteenth and the beginning of the nineteenth century:

Miss Doucet, at the sign of the Gland d'Or, in the Arcade of the Palais Royal.

Prévot, in the Palais Royal, near the Café du Caveau.

Dufour, in the Arcade of the Palais Royal.

Lecompte, clothier in the Palais Royal who had the monopoly for selling the famous 'Monuments of Paris' underglass buttons.

Foucault, at the sign of the Ville de Bordeaux, rue St Honoré.

Roffart, at the sign of the Bras d'Or, rue de la Ferronnerie.

Huline, at the sign of the Ville de Londres, rue de la Ferronnerie.

During the Empire Period, four Parisian buttonmakers were very busy making buttons for the Imperial Army:

André Christophe, Rue des Enfants Rouges.

Feuillet, 2 Rue des Petits Champs.

J. S. Hericée, 52 Rue Bourg l'Abbé.

Houssement, 14 Rue de la Chaudière, supplier to H.M. the Emperor Napoléon 1 and the Imperial Guard.

PASSEMENTERIE BUTTONS

THESE are dress buttons, embroidered by needle or crochet and sometimes decorated with beads or braids, which appeared for the first time in France during the fourteenth century. French records of the time mention the existence of *passementiers* who were allowed to embroider fabrics, braids and buttons. The corporation statutes of 1559 mention that the said *passementiers* were allowed to make,

Buttons matching the trimmings of this 18th-century coat.

among other things, at least seven types of *passementerie* buttons (*à poires, glands, vases, olives, piqués, jaserons*). France remained the main producer of this type of button, the peak period being the eighteenth century, when the buttons matched the trimmings on dresses or coats worn by the nobility. They were made well into the nineteenth century, and important centres of production were in the Vosges region and in the Oise departement, nearer Paris. Some of them were adorned with various materials such as jet, steel, sequins, pearls, gold, silver and even mother-of-pearl. A kind of *passementerie* button decorated with beads was produced in the nineteenth century.

PASTE OR STRASS BUTTONS

THE name 'paste' or 'strass' is given to lead-glass cut into the form of gemstones, the latter name being that of Georges Frederic Strass,

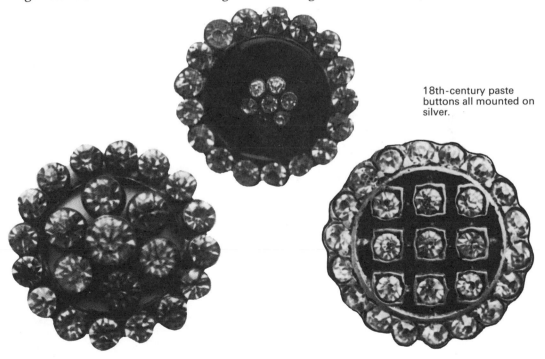

18th-century paste buttons all mounted on silver.

Above: A set of early 19th-century buttons mounted in silver, decorated in enamel and paste (strass). Collection A. Wittamer, Brussels.

Left and centre: 19th-century French buttons mounted on silver and decorated with paste and encrusted blue enamels.

Right: 19th-century paste button mounted on metal and decorated with cut steel facets, in the fashion of the last quarter of the century.

from Strasbourg, a goldsmith on the Quai des Orfèvres in Paris, who perfected the technique of making paste 'gems' around 1734. The Egyptians, however, had also used the technique and the art persisted in Italy throughout the Middle Ages up to the Renaissance. English jewellers adopted the technique and called it paste (from the Italian 'pasta', meaning pastry): the glassmakers of Uttoxeter and Bristol were the first to make these imitation stones in the eighteenth century, hence the name 'Bristol stone'. Many paste buttons have been manufactured up to the present day. The antique versions, always backed in silver, were often made from a single piece of metal with holes drilled in it and small silver cups soldered behind to hold the stones, but in many nineteenth- and twentieth-century paste buttons the stones are only cemented into place. The old stones, with the passing years, have acquired a yellowish tint. Other gems besides diamonds have been copied, particularly topaz and amethysts, but never rubies.

Beautiful paste button of unusual shape mounted on silver.

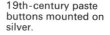

19th-century paste buttons mounted on silver.

PATENT OFFICE REGISTRATION MARK

SOME British buttons manufactured between 1842 and 1883 carry a diamond-mark which indicates that the design was registered with the British Patent Office. Where a button carries such a mark but the manufacturer's name does not appear, it is sometimes possible to obtain the missing information by writing to the Comptroller, Patent

Office, 25 Southampton Building, London WC 2. The patent mark enables one to ascertain the day, month and year when the patent was registered. The patent mark has been found on ceramic, horn and metal buttons.

PEWTER BUTTONS

NO one knows who first had the idea of manufacturing pewter buttons. The alloy has been known in Europe since Roman times and pewter was widely used from the middle of the fourteenth century until at least the beginning of the nineteenth century. As the pewter buttons found today are never marked, they are, of course, difficult to date. Pewter buttons were made throughout the eighteenth century in every country of Europe, particularly for men's clothes. There was a revival of popularity around 1850, but this was short-lived. The oldest pewter buttons seem to have been made in moulds of stone or metal, in the form of one-piece buttons with a self-shank. Only the pewter buttons manufactured after 1800 have an iron shank. Pewter buttons are still made. Those made by Den Norske Knappefabrik, in Littlehammer, Norway, are very attractive and decorated with Scandinavian motifs.

Very large 18th-century Flemish pewter button showing the lion of Flanders.

90

PICTURE BUTTONS

PICTURE buttons, the easiest category for the collector to find, started appearing in Europe, mainly in France, around 1875. Their production ceased at the start of the First World War. Everything and anything can be found represented on picture buttons, with subjects taken from fables, stories, mythology, religion, transport,

Late 19th-century picture buttons depicting various means of transport. The aircraft button is plated silver, and shows *Ilbis*, the first plane to cross the Channel, in 1909.

Picture buttons of medieval inspiration.

91

the Far East, songs, zoology, ornithology, operas and operettas, the circus, architecture, inanimate objects, games and the theatre. They were nearly all made in stamped brass or cheaper metals, in the form of a two-piece button. Some of the scenes represented, however, are difficult to identify accurately.

Set of 19th-century
stamped metal
storybuttons.

Metal picture buttons of the 19th century of medieval inspiration.

19th-century picture buttons with Chaldean designs.

Two 19th-century picture buttons, in stamped metal, of Roman design.

PINCHBECK BUTTONS

PINCHBECK is an alloy of copper and zinc, sometimes washed with gold, and named after its inventors Christopher Pinchbeck and his son Edward, well-known clockmakers in London during the first half of the eighteenth century. The Pinchbecks themselves made and sold buttons of this alloy. Pinchbeck was widely used during the eighteenth century to make shoe buckles, watch chains and all kinds of small boxes as well as buttons, and was sometimes plated with a thin layer of gold. The most attractive buttons of this type were made by Matthew Boulton of Birmingham.

PLAYING CARDS

PLAYING cards have inspired more than one buttonmaker, especially in France during the eighteenth century, when miniature cards were painted on paper or ivory and inserted in underglass buttons. Cards can also be found on cheap metal picture buttons from the last quarter of the nineteenth century.

POLIN, JACQUES

JACQUES Polin, a Parisian goldsmith active in the sixteenth century, had premises on the well-known Pont au Change. François I ordered from him 13,600 gold buttons 'to be sewn on a black velvet dress'.

PORCELAIN BUTTONS

French porcelain button of the first World War with the photograph of French soldier.

BUTTONS made of porcelain are among the most attractive of all buttons, but they are also the most fragile. Millions of porcelain buttons have been made but few have survived and they are very rare today. It has been established that Sèvres and Tournai made some buttons in soft paste porcelain as early as the eighteenth century; but it is still very doubtful that Meissen produced buttons at that time, and it seems that in fact Copenhagen was then making more porcelain buttons, in hard paste, than any other European factory. The rarest porcelain buttons are those which bear the mark of the factory on the reverse side (providing the mark is authentic). Many buttons of unknown origin bear the so-called crossed swords of Meissen and the two L's of Sèvres, but they are fake. Most of the porcelain buttons found today were made during the nineteenth

Very rare 18th-century French buttons of hand painted porcelain, mounted under glass in copper frames.

Five Minton porcelain buttons manufactured 1850.

century, the first being produced by R. Prosser, Birmingham buttonmaker, in 1840, in collaboration with the Minton factory. The famous Wedgwood buttons are in jasperware, not porcelain. The Prosser monopoly lasted only a few years, until 1850, when the

Coalport porcelain button made in Shropshire c.1850. Handpainted flower design in pink, yellow and white. Mounted in silver.
Private collection.

European porcelain buttons. 19th century.

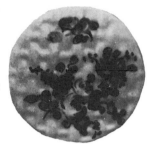

European porcelain buttons: left: French Louis XVI style mounted on silver. Right: early 19th century.

Maison Bapterosses, in Briare, Montereau and Paris, took up the challenge and started producing porcelain buttons of all types which, in fact, flooded the market. A very interesting type of porcelain button is the 'Liverpool' or Liverpool transfer button (see entry p. 73). The name does not mean that the buttons were produced in Liverpool, some being marked 'Paris', and their origin has not been definitely established, but they are quite beautiful,

Extremely rare set of eight porcelain buttons decorated with scenes representing the four seasons. They are transfer-printed with the exception of the gold background, which is handpainted. Probably French, 19th century.

always mounted on metal, and decorated by transfer, usually featuring classical heads. They all date from the second half of the nineteenth century. The Coalport factory also produced some good quality porcelain buttons, but it would appear they were all made around 1900 and later. Porcelain buttons are still produced in Europe and some beautiful 'fakes' have been made in Limoges, mainly for the tourist trade. (See also entries under Copenhagen Porcelain p. 94, and Tournai p. 123.)

PORNOGRAPHY

QUITE a number of pornographic buttons have been produced through the centuries, mainly in France at the end of the eighteenth century, notably in Paris, where shops displayed sets of thirty buttons, for example, depicting scenes from the works of Aretine, the famous Italian sixteenth-century writer. Such buttons would fetch a very high price today. The buttons were quite successful and certain painters, such as the miniaturist Klingstedt, specialised in them. The Swiss enameller Thouron and a certain François Laîné produced some very erotic scenes. Around 1775, buttons with a double switch were also produced, allowing the owner to show the pornographic scene only on request. Buttons of this type were also produced in Japan and in India, where large ivory buttons were sold hand-painted with *risque* scenes.

PORTRAIT BUTTONS

19th-century button with the head of Minerva in brass applied to a background of brown leather.

ANY number of historical or fictional characters have inspired buttonmakers throughout the centuries and this type of button can be the object of one single collection. In the eighteenth century, for example, a very rare set of underglass buttons was produced, featuring the heads of all the French revolutionaries. During the Empire Period there were sets showing beautiful women, among them Pauline, Napoleon's sister, painted on ivory. But most buttons of this type belong to the period of the picture buttons, in the second half of the nineteenth century, when hundreds of people were represented on stamped metal buttons: Napoleon, Joan of Arc, Queen Victoria, William Tell, Rembrandt, Beethoven, Lincoln,

Lafayette, various queens and kings, Washington, etc. Hundreds of unidentified ladies appear on eighteenth-century underglass buttons and it would be impossible to cite all the buttons featuring heads from classical history—Hector, Achilles and Cleopatra are among the common ones. Collectors might concentrate on eighteenth-century underglass and nineteenth-century silver buttons of this type.

Silver portrait button of Andreas Hofer, leader of the Tyrolean revolt against the Bavarian Government. Early 19th century.

Left: Silver button with bronze border depicting Mary Queen of Scots. 19th century.

Two 19th-century buttons, in stamped metal, showing the great Greek warrior Achilles.

99

Left: Dutch silver button with the head of Queen Wilhelmina of the Netherlands when she was young.

Centre: Napoleon Bonaparte on a stamped metal button.

Right: Stamped metal button from the end of the 19th century showing the head of Ludwig von Beethoven.

PREHISTORIC AND ANTIQUE BUTTONS

OBJECTS in the form of buttons have been excavated in Egypt, in Persia, and in Greece. Schliemann found buttons among the treasures of Mycenae and Troy. Apart from those found in Greece, it would appear that the most ancient European button, made of bronze between 1400 and 1200 BC, is one attached to the so-called Muldberg costume in the National Museum in Copenhagen. An antique button in gold was found in the Herculaneum excavations, and the Louvre Museum in Paris has a beautiful button in metal plated with gold which comes from a tomb in the Megara Acropolis and was probably made about 650 BC. But although buttons were apparently used by the Egyptians, the Greeks and the Persians of ancient times, no mention of them has been found in any document before the twelfth century. It is very rare today to find prehistoric or antique buttons.

PUNCH BUTTONS

PUNCH, the English humorous magazine, has always been famous for its cartoons and drawings. Twelve of those drawings, published between 1844 and 1849, were reproduced on stamped brass buttons and quickly became collectors' items.

RAFFIA BUTTONS

IT is not known when raffia buttons were first made, but it would appear that the German button industry produced some during the nineteenth century and continued to do so into the twentieth century, until the period after the Second World War. Although raffia buttons are comparatively rare, they are never very old. Most of these beautiful buttons were made of pieces of raffia stretched over a mounting in metal.

REALISTICS

BUTTONS made in realistic shapes appeared in great numbers in the 1920s, but realistics had been made well before that time. They were moulded in various types of material and also carved in wood. The oldest among the twentieth-century production are of glass, which was later replaced by plastic. Many collectors scorn those buttons made for children which were sold for a few pence in the department stores of the thirties, but not everyone can afford to buy rare eighteenth-century buttons and collecting realistics could be an amusing and rewarding pastime. Millions of them have been thrown away over the years, but they are still to be found without great difficulty.

Realistic glass buttons manufactured in the thirties. The head is probably that of Josephine Baker, the well known singer. This type of button, very attractive and still plentiful, was originally made for children.

REBUS BUTTONS

A *REBUS* is a name, or phrase, made up of pictures which pun with parts of the word. The *rebus* button, in ivory or in mother-of-pearl, flat and very large, was made in Paris at the end of the eighteenth century to please the younger generation of the time, the *rebus* being engraved or painted on the background. Anyone who speaks French can understand the *rebuses*: they consist mostly of short sentences of an amorous nature such as were exchanged by lovers. The rarest are mounted on metal, the *rebus* being painted in reverse on the covering glass.

101

REPOUSSÉ

REPOUSSÉ describes a very ancient technique used by jewellers and goldsmiths to hammer any type of metal into relief, the pattern being pressed from the back, giving the impression of embossing. Genuine *repoussé* buttons are very rare, but many stamped buttons in metal give the impression of the *repoussé* technique.

REVERSE PAINTING

THIS is a very ancient Chinese art of painting scenes or figures at the back of a piece of glass. Many eighteenth-century French underglass buttons were decorated in this way, the background usually being formed by an ivory disc. Some nineteenth-century buttons of this type also exist. They are smaller but just as rare as their eighteenth-century counterparts.

Two French 18th-century underglass buttons painted in reverse with representations of birds.

REVOLUTIONARY BUTTONS

THE French Revolution of 1789 inspired the Parisian buttonmakers to produce much sought-after revolutionary buttons, which illustrated the ideas of the revolution and were, in fact, a form of propaganda in their own right. The most beautiful are of the underglass type, decorated with engravings or drawings of revolutionary scenes such as the storming of the Bastille. Others carry revolutionary slogans such as: 'I am tired of carrying them' (the sword of the nobility and the clerical cross), 'The sun shines for all', or 'I safeguard the nation'. Some scenes were painted on paper, some on ivory and some even on silk. To the confusion of today's collectors, a lot of them were reproduced in France during the nineteenth century and even later, including some made of enamel. Those copied most were buttons in stamped brass, which were worn by the revolutionary soldiers and a collection of which is in the *Musée des Invalides* in Paris. A representation of the guillotine has never been discovered on a button.

RUBBER BUTTONS

STRANGE as it may seem, there were buttons made of rubber in the last half of the nineteenth century, most of them with the name Goodyear as backmark and sometimes Patt. or Patent 1851, the year in which Nelson Goodyear obtained a patent to protect a process discovered to improve the manufacture of hard rubber, or India rubber. Nelson Goodyear, brother of the inventor Charles Goodyear, who discovered the process of vulcanisation in 1839, improved upon his brother's invention.

America produced many rubber buttons in practically all shapes, usually black with wire shanks or self shanks. This type of button is difficult to find in Europe, for, according to some documents kept in the Birmingham Reference Library, Europeans objected to the smell of the buttons and they never became popular this side of the Atlantic.

RUSKIN POTTERY

FIRM of potters in Smethwick, about forty miles south of Birmingham. It is known to have made pottery buttons in the early twentieth century, decorated with coloured glazes.

SAMPLE CARDS

FROM the beginning of the nineteenth century, commercial travellers selling buttons to retailers, took sample cards with them.

Complete sets of buttons of different colours and sizes were displayed on these cards, which bore the manufacturer's name or, more often, the fanciful name of the collection.

The buttons bought were delivered either on cards or in bulk in cardboard boxes, usually with names which make it almost impossible to identify their origin. The names were almost always written in French. French buttonmakers of the second part of the nineteenth century complained bitterly about such names as *'Modes de Paris'*, *'Boutons de Paris'*, *'Nouveautés de Paris'* or *'Nouveautés Françaises'* printed on cards and boxes by foreign manufacturers. Following official complaints, many consignments of foreign buttons were seized by the French police. Sample cards of the nineteenth century are much sought after today and some are valuable finds.

SANDERS, B.

SANDERS, a Dane by origin, became a buttonmaker in Birmingham at the beginning of the nineteenth century, immediately after the bombardment of Copenhagen by the British fleet under Nelson. His claim to fame is that he invented a cloth button with a metal shank. His son, B. Sanders Junior, followed his father as manager of the business and invented the flexible shank button. Military buttons equipped with the Sanders-type shank, yet another improvement (see Shanks p. 105), are still quite easy to find.

SCRIMSHAW BUTTONS

THESE buttons, made from the teeth and bones of whales or the tusks of walrus, were hand-carved by sailors on whaling ships. After carving, they were usually polished and designs were scratched into them. Sometimes black or brightly coloured ink was rubbed into the incised lines. Most scrimshaw buttons date from the nineteenth century.

SECRET COMPARTMENT BUTTONS

THESE buttons, which are difficult to find, were designed as, or made into lockets to hold the photograph of a loved one or some other precious object. The most ancient locket buttons known were made in Paris during the reign of Louis XVI and contained tiny pornographic scenes. During the nineteenth century, and again during World War I, many buttons were made into lockets to keep photographs from curious eyes. One type in particular, which may still be found occasionally, was made for the Royal Air Force aircrews at the beginning of the Second World War. It contained a tiny compass intended to aid aircrews shot down over enemy territory. The idea was adopted by the United States Air Force when the USA joined the war. Its secret was never discovered by the Germans. This famous RAF compass button was invented by a Major Clayton-Hutton, and manufactured by the Birmingham firm of J. R. Gaunt, Warstone Parade, Birmingham.

SÈVRES

THE soft paste porcelain factory founded in Vincennes in 1738 was transferred to Sèvres, its present location, in 1753. Quite a number of buttons are to be found bearing an imitation of the Sèvres mark; but usually these are buttons made by various factories in Paris, and knowledgeable collectors of china are rarely deceived by them. Sèvres, however, did produce buttons, though in very small quantity. The Sèvres records mention two deliveries of buttons, one in 1787, the other in 1789. The first delivery was of twenty-eight buttons, sold for 120 pounds to a certain M. Lenormand d'Etioles. The other was of eight buttons for a watch-chain, sold for six pounds. The Sèvres records covering the nineteenth century mention only a few sales of shirt buttons. Around 1925, Sèvres also produced a few cuff-buttons.

SHANKS

MOST buttons produced throughout the centuries have been equipped with shanks, but they do not always give an indication of the period from which they date. The cone shank was used during the eighteenth century and at the beginning of the nineteenth, and all buttons equipped with it can be considered to be antique. A number of eighteenth-century buttons were also equipped, however, with the Alpha-type shank which is still in use today. The Sanders-type shank, which has been used for billions of buttons made all over the world, indicates only that the button was not made before about 1825. Most of the shanks one finds today are of nineteenth-century vintage, with the exception, of course, of the Alpha-type and the cone-type. Most moulded buttons, like those made of celluloid, horn, plastic and glass, have a shank which is part of the button and is therefore referred to as a self-shank.

Some buttons manufactured between 1830 and the First World War were simply made with what is now called a thread-back, where threads have been wound over and across the back of the button, appearing to radiate from the centre. Many collectors discard these buttons because the thread is usually now well-worn.

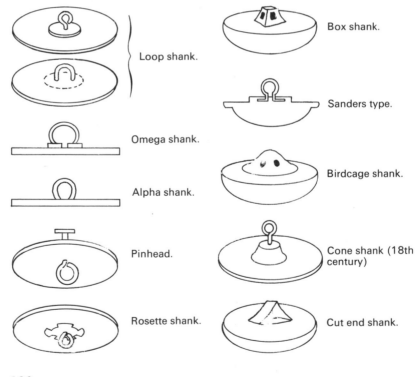

Loop shank.

Box shank.

Omega shank.

Sanders type.

Alpha shank.

Birdcage shank.

Pinhead.

Cone shank (18th century)

Rosette shank.

Cut end shank.

SHEFFIELD PLATE

SHEFFIELD plate is not plate in the sense commonly accepted by collectors and it was not made only in Sheffield, as might be assumed. The plating of silver in ancient and medieval times was done by grafting thin slivers or sheets of silver on to an already made-up piece. Sheffield plate is made by the process discovered by Thomas Boulsover around the year 1750. The discovery was accidental, when Boulsover noticed that silver and copper could be fused together so firmly that it was impossible to part them. When put through a rolling mill the two fused metals expanded in unison and behaved as one metal. It was therefore possible to create a sheet of base metal covered with a skin of silver and use it to make articles of certain required shapes exactly as if one were working with a single metal. According to Boulsover's obituary published in the *Derby Mercury* on 17 September 1788, the inventor 'commenced a manufacture (in Sheffield plate) of plated snuff-boxes and buttons'. However, real Sheffield buttons are very difficult to identify and many collectors give the name to any buttons which are silver-plated. Other well known manufacturers of 'fused plate' were Joseph Hancock, Thomas Law—another Master of the Sheffield Cutlers—and the firm Tudor and Leader. Other names are Jacob and Samuel Roberts, Thomas Bradbury (a firm which lasted into the twentieth century), Winter, Ashford Ellis and Co. and Matthew Fenton and Co. Sheffield plate was soon made in other cities, notably in Birmingham where Matthew Boulton became very quickly the largest single manufacturer of fused plate in Britain. Sheffield plate was also manufactured in Nottingham and London, as well as in France, Russia and, possibly, Germany.

SILK WOVEN BUTTONS

A NUMBER of silk woven buttons were produced during the nineteenth century in France, Great Britain and Switzerland, and quite probably in other countries. These buttons were made on what is known as a Jacquard loom, after the mechanic Joseph-Marie Jacquard from Lyons, who invented it. They are incorrectly called Stevengraph buttons in the United States, after Thomas Stevens, the well known Coventry manufacturer, although it is not even known that Stevens ever produced buttons. The idea of producing woven silk novelties, such as ribbons, bookmarks, and pictures, seems to be continental rather than English. In fact, manufacturers such as François Carquillat and Potton Rainbaud, both of Lyons, made silk-woven novelties before Stevens, but most of the early French production was in black and different shades of grey, while the Coventry manufacturers produced their novelties in bright colours. The two Swiss firms of Kelchlin & Sons and Wahl & Svein, of Basle, made silk novelties as early as the middle of the nineteenth century. Of all the numerous Coventry manufacturers, it is only known for a certainty that William Henry Grant, main competitor of Thomas Stevens, produced silk-woven buttons at the end of the nineteenth century. It is quite likely that similar buttons were produced in other countries but, as they are not marked, identification is difficult.

Silk machine-embroidered button of the so-called Stevengraph type.

SILVER BUTTONS

INDICATIONS are that the first silver buttons were made in England and France at the beginning of the sixteenth century, but those very early pieces are rarely found. The oldest silver buttons one can normally hope to find today were produced during the eighteenth century, when they became fashionable all over Europe, the most commonly found being hunting and livery buttons (see entries p. 63 and p. 74). A collector could, however, be lucky enough to

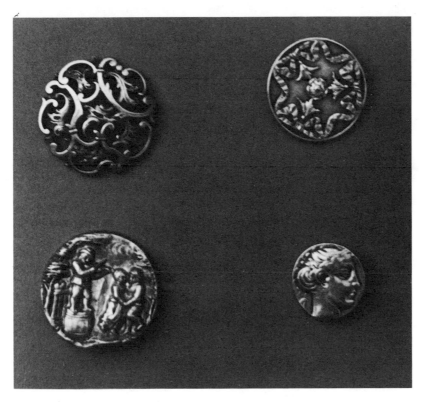

find one of the beautiful Dutch silver buttons, some six centimetres in diameter, which Dutch silversmiths made as early as the seventeenth century. They feature scenes from the Old and New Testament in *repoussé* work, scenes illustrating the different months, hunting scenes, and pictures of those handsome ships which made Holland prosperous. These buttons were sometimes used as money by Dutch sailors and merchants overseas, or were kept in the same family for generations. Silver buttons have been made everywhere, in Sweden, Norway, Italy, Austria and Russia, and they are still being made. Even when gilt buttons appeared at the beginning of the nineteenth century, silver buttons continued to be made and silver was used to mount all kinds of decoration on buttons, including paste and enamel, fancy jewels and glass. In Birmingham, two firms

French silver buttons. 19th century.

were well known for their silver buttons during the nineteenth century, J. H. Cutler of Newton Road, and Barwell of James Street, who was famous not only for his gold buttons, but also for Maltese buttons made of glass mounted on gold or silver. One type of silver button which is fairly easy to find today is the Highland dress button (see p. 61), occasionally made in Scotland, but most often in Birmingham. Another type is the breast-shaped silver button made in Bergen, in Norway, also during the nineteenth century. Unfortunately for collectors, although all silver buttons made in Britain are hallmarked, most of the others are not, except some made in Russia, Norway and Holland. Buttons have not been hallmarked in France since 1822.

SKULL BUTTONS

A SKULL button is always a rare find, although these buttons were very fashionable in France at the end of the sixteenth century in the reign of Henri III, who is reputed to have started the craze on the death of one of his favourites. In the accounts of the French Court for 1585, there is an entry reading: 'Eighteen dozens of big silver buttons, decorated with skulls, for dresses, at two *écus* a dozen'.

SLATE BUTTONS

A CERTAIN number of buttons, now very rare indeed, have been made from slate. Some experiments, which were not very successful, were carried out in France in the nineteenth century, in the region of Renazé in the province of Mayenne, but most slate buttons were manufactured by the firm Clay's in England, during the same period.

SMITH, KEMP AND WRIGHT LTD

THIS is a well known button-making firm founded in Birmingham in the 1840s, when its name first appears in the local directories. Its premises were in Brearley Street West. From the 1850s the firm appears to have enjoyed a solid reputation for specialising in silver-plated buttons 'such as those used for police clothing . . .'. They were made of copper and silvered on one side only, the inner side retaining its copper colour. In the latter part of the nineteenth century the firm started producing other types of button made of horn and bone, ivory and mother-of-pearl, papier mâché, steel, enamel, zinc, glass, wood and pearl. The firm is still in existence today at 15, Brearley Street, Birmingham 19.

SNAKESKIN BUTTONS

SNAKESKIN buttons are by no means antique. They were manufactured on a very small scale after the beginning of the twentieth century, to match other accessories such as handbags, shoes or belts. Snakeskin buttons do not attract the attention of collectors as they are only curiosities, at least at present.

SPA BUTTONS

THE small Belgian town of Spa, which claims to have given its name to all other thermal spas in the world, started attracting visitors in the sixteenth century. Since then the town's inhabitants have

Very rare Spa button in wood, handpainted with flowers and covered with a coat of the special Spa varnish invented in the 18th century. *c.*1860.

manufactured all kinds of trinkets in wood, engraved or hand painted, to sell to the cure-taking visitors. Between 1850 and 1860 they produced sets of beautiful hand-painted buttons in wood, round or oval in shape and decorated usually with flowers. They were covered by a thin coat of Spa varnish.

SPORTING BUTTONS

SPORTING buttons differ from hunting buttons in that they do not picture hunting scenes, hunters, or their prey, but scenes or symbols of sporting activities such as rowing, fishing, football, cycling, tennis, and boxing. They date from about 1850.

19th century French sporting buttons in stamped metal.

SPORTING JEWELLERY BUTTONS

English sporting jewellery button.

INEXPENSIVE jewellery for men, decorated with sporting subjects such as birds, horses, dogs, and foxes, bacame fashionable just after 1850. They included tie-pins, cuff-links, studs and buttons. They were made of 'Essex crystal', cabochon cut-rock crystal, painted on the back. The buttons were all small and intended only for waistcoats.

STEEL BUTTONS

STEEL was used to make buttons from the middle of the eighteenth

112

French 18th-century steel buttons from a very rare set of twelve, with applied ormolu figures in high relief.

century up to about 1830, and again in the last quarter of the nineteenth century, when cut steel facets were used to decorate buttons made of other material. The eighteenth-century buttons are easily identified as they are usually very large, always flat and of simple design. The invention of the steel button is credited by most historians to Matthew Boulton, the Birmingham industrialist, who made Birmingham the centre of the British button industry. Around 1745 Matthew Boulton started replacing precious and semi-precious stones used in jewellery by cut steel facets which were riveted to flat steel discs. The term 'cut steel' refers only to buttons which are entirely made of facets, some having up to 150 pieces arranged in concentric circles. The first Boulton steel buttons were made only to

113

order, but the fashion took hold around 1860 and spread rapidly all over the British Isles and then to the Continent. The French buttonmaker Dauffe, whose shop was in the Faubourg St. Antoines in Paris, is reputed to have started the fashion there about 1775. He was already a firm believer in advertising, as we can read in the *Journal de Paris* dated 8 July 1787, when he announced: '. . . a set of coat buttons, decorated with pearls and riveted diamonds, all in steel'. The French buttonmakers improved upon the English designs and some of the most attractive are composed of a flat steel disc, often engraved, on to which beautiful bronze designs were riveted. The eighteenth-century buttons have a diameter of about 3.5 cm. and

114

18th-century steel button entirely made up of cut steel facets and covered with a coat of black lacquer.

Beautiful 19th-century cut steel button decorated with paste.

more, while those made in the first quarter of the nineteenth century, although much smaller in size, are more decorative and usually domed. The cut steel facets, when they came into fashion again in the late nineteenth century, were often set in filigree frames to give a lace-like effect, or riveted to buttons made in enamel, wood, brass and other metals, not to mention ivory, tortoiseshell, bone and even mother-of-pearl. After 1890 the individually riveted cut-steel facets gave way to thin sheets of metal which were stamped into facets. Eighteenth-century steel buttons, which were really made to last, are still plentiful.

19th-century filigree button decorated with cut steel facets.

19th-century buttons in metal decorated with steel facets.

115

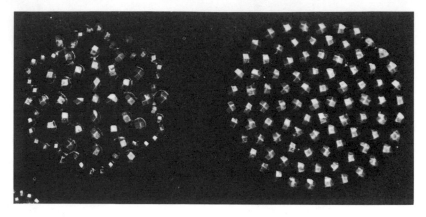

18th-century cut steel buttons probably of English origin.

STORY BUTTONS

THESE buttons, which may be seen as a category of picture buttons, are mostly in stamped metal and date from the last quarter of the nineteenth century. They illustrate fables, nursery rhymes, childhood stories, operas and plays, stories from the Bible etc., many

Buttons illustrating stories became fashionable during the 19th century, mainly in England, France and Germany. Themes include classical legends, fables and fairy stories, often in stamped metal.

116

of which can be clearly identified today. Among common examples are pictures of Red Riding Hood, Puss in Boots, the Fox and the Crow, Don Quixote, St George and the Dragon, Rebecca at the Well and Madame Butterfly. In other cases however it is more difficult to identify the stories concerned.

The value of story buttons, or in fact any type of picture button, depends not only on the picture itself, but the size of the button, as most of these buttons were manufactured in four or five sizes. It is fair to say that the value of such buttons is normally in direct proportion to their size.

SULPHIDES

THESE buttons are the rarest of all. The first objects made by this process were not buttons but jewellery and appeared originally in Bohemia around 1750, and later in Paris during the reign of Louis XVI, where Parisian glassmakers improved upon the process. A certain Desprez was making them in his workshop at 2 Rue des Recollets at the end of the eighteenth century. Known today as crystallo-ceramic or glass-encrusted cameos, sulphides were made

Sulphide buttons made by the English glassmaker Aspley Pellatt at the beginning of the 19th century. As far as is known, they are the only Pellatt buttons in existence. Reproduced by kind permission of Birmingham City Museums and Art Gallery.

first with a steatite paste which acquired a kind of silvery frost when put in contact with the melted crystal. British makers followed with Aspley Pellatt, then with John Ford and even with the Ridways, the Staffordshire potters. Aspley Pellatt made some beautiful pieces in his Falcon Glasshouse, at Southwark, as did John Ford, in his Holyrood Glass Works in Edinburgh, following in the footsteps of James Tassie who experimented at the end of the eighteenth century. Sulphide buttons have been found, but it is rather difficult to identify the maker. It is probable that the French glassworks of the Gros Gaillou, Baccarat, St Louis and, later, Clichy, made them, as well as various British manufacturers. The only sulphide buttons which were definitely made by Pellatt are now in the Birmingham Museum.

SWASTIKA BUTTONS

THE Nazis of the Third Reich used the swastika as their main decorative theme, but they seem seldom to have placed it on their buttons. Swastika buttons are not easy to find, though a particularly good quality button decorated with a German Eagle carrying a swastika does exist. The back mark indicates that the manufacturer used a vaguely Gothic 'A' as his symbol. They were made in different sizes and are also marked *'Extra Fein'*.

Two types of Nazi buttons, one worn by party members, the other by civilians. The armed forces never had swastikas on their buttons.

118

SYNTHETICS

AFTER about 1874 many buttons were manufactured with the new plastics. Although they can, of course, be collected, most serious European collectors disregard them, except perhaps buttons made in celluloid. Celluloid was the first plastic which was widely used for making buttons. It appears to have been invented by the Englishman Parker around the year 1855, but was 'rediscovered' and commercialised by the Hyatt brothers in New York in 1865. The first celluloid buttons appeared only about 1875, the new plastic being processed to imitate many materials, including glass, paper, ivory, mother-of-pearl and wood. Hundreds of different types of buttons have been made out of celluloid, the only choice ones being in embossed celluloid made to look like ivory. Following the discovery of casein by the Frenchman Trillat in 1891 and that of galatlithe (milk-stone) by the Germans Krische and Spitteler in 1897, billions of plastic buttons were manufactured. Their advent really marked the end of an era. The Belgian chemist Leon Hendrik Baekeland,

Above and below: Celluloid buttons, end of 19th century.

119

working in the United States, discovered bakelite between 1907 and 1909, although not many buttons were made in it. None of these buttons, nor their newer counterparts, can really be regarded as collectors' items.

TAYLOR, JOHN

TAYLOR was the first important buttonmaker of Birmingham, later also High Sheriff of Warwickshire (1756). He founded what can probably be called the first real factory in Birmingham, in the 1730s, where he employed more than 500 people and achieved a weekly turnover of some £800. He is reputed to have greatly improved the different processes of making gilt buttons, which were a speciality of Birmingham in the second half of the eighteenth century. He also started making buttons and other articles in japanned ware in the manner of the Pontypool craftsmen.

THREAD-BACKS

THESE buttons have, in place of a proper shank, crisscross threads radiating from the centre. Buttons with thread-backs were made in glass, tôle (thin sheet iron), or other metal and all date from the nineteenth century.

THREE-FOLD LINEN BUTTONS

IN 1841 John Aston, buttonmaker in Birmingham, patented the invention by a certain Humphrey Jeffries of a three-fold linen button, a ring of metal encased in linen in such a way that both sides and centre are covered with separate pieces of material and thus produced quite flat. This type of button superseded in Britain the old thread-button of Dorset (see p. 38).

TOGGLE BUTTONS

TOGGLE buttons of various types have been manufactured from at least the middle of the sixteenth century, up to the beginning of the twentieth. The original toggle button, which is a very rare early

120

fastener, mostly of German or Dutch origin, was a very elaborate ball-shaped silver button connected to a thin bar by means of a link. Later, from the seventeenth century on, toggle buttons were made, mainly in Holland, consisting of a flat one- or two-piece silver button attached to a link and a bar. And later still, the toggle button consisted of two buttons connected with each other by a small chain, the buttons being either of the same size or of two different sizes.

This last type of button was made as late as the nineteenth century on the Continent. It often comprised two glass balls fitted with regulation shanks, joined together by a small chain; but beautiful enamel toggle buttons in *fin-de-siècle* style have also been found—these buttons of course must not be confused with cuff-links. Ancient toggle buttons are very scarce nowadays and are therefore very valuable finds. In Dutch families, they have traditionally been handed down from one generation to another.

TÔLEWARE BUTTONS

KNOWN in France and in the USA as painted *tôle,* these buttons are

121

known in England as japanned tinware. Painted *tôle* buttons are of thin sheet-iron coated with lacquer and painted over in the manner of the painted enamels. The process of lacquering metal was known in Bohemia as long ago as the fourteenth century, but it was perfected in Wales by a certain Edward Algood of Pontypool. The making of japanned tinware was taken over later by craftsmen in Wolverhampton and Birmingham, who continued to call their ware 'Pontypool'. It is probable that buttons of this type were also made in France, Germany and Holland. They are covered with black, chocolate-brown or red lacquer and usually painted with oriental motifs. For some reason the production of painted *tôle* was discontinued everywhere around 1860.

TORTOISESHELL BUTTONS

TORTOISESHELL buttons are very rare indeed, as their production in Europe has always been restricted: the shells had to come from as far away as the China Seas and the coasts of the Philippines, India and America. But tortoiseshell has been used in Europe to make various objects since the beginning of the sixteenth century, the

Left: Tortoiseshell sew-through button of the 19th century decorated with a border of paste.

Right: Very rare Scottish tortoiseshell button of the 19th century decorated with a thistle in silver on a silk background.

122

French appearing to have been the first to learn how to work with it. Some tortoiseshell buttons were left undecorated, the natural beauty of the shell being considered enough, but a very few have been inlaid with gold or silver, and others decorated with a border of paste or pearls. Some buttons were made in artificial tortoiseshell of a deep red colour, an invention attributed to a Frenchman, Darcet, who was active at the beginning of the nineteenth century.

TOURNAI

TOURNAI was the site of a well known Belgian porcelain factory founded in 1750. It rivalled the Sèvres factory and produced beautiful pieces in soft paste porcelain until about 1830. Buttons in soft paste porcelain were produced in Tournai in very small quantities during the eighteenth century. They were usually decorated by hand with a gold border and featured various birds or idyllic country scenes in the manner of the eighteenth-century French painters. The diameter of these buttons is always 3.7 cm.

These beautiful soft paste porcelain buttons were produced, probably on a limited scale, by the Tournai manufactory, at the end of the 18th century. Reproduced by permission of A.C.L., Brussels.

123

TOURNELLES (HENRI LE SEQ DES)

FRENCH collector of steel jewellery, whose collection, rich in buttons, was assembled during the second part of the nineteenth century. It is now exhibited in the Tournelles Museum, formerly the church of St Laurent, in Rouen.

TWIGG G. AND CO.

A NUMBER of button manufacturers of the name of Twigg appear in early nineteenth-century Birmingham trade directories. G. Twigg, of Powell Street, first appears in 1849 and seems to have been connected with William Twigg of 12 James Street. The records of 1853 mention Messrs Twigg of James Street and Powell Street as being makers of glass buttons. Their buttons were produced mainly for waistcoats, some of the glass beads being imported from Bohemia. By 1855 the firm had become Twigg and Silvester, of Powell Street. It also produced military, livery, sporting and steel buttons.

VEGETABLE IVORY OR 'COROZO' BUTTONS

THE corozo, which was used to make billions of buttons during the second part of the nineteenth century, is a nut which grows on a certain type of palm tree, the Phytelepah, found mainly in Peru and in Equador. The first buttons of this material, in many ways precursors of the plastic button, were exhibited in the English section of the Universal Exhibition of 1862 in London. English buttonmakers seem to have been well ahead of their French rivals who started making them in 1870. Normally, corozo (or vegetable ivory) buttons are white, but some were dyed yellow or amber. The grain of the corozo nut being very tight, the dyes did not penetrate very well, with the result that the colour has rubbed off most of the dyed buttons found today. Collectors of this cheap type of button can find many specimens which have been engraved, stamped, stencil-decorated, painted and even transfer-decorated. Some are decorated with metal escutcheons or embellished by the addition of cut steel facets.

Corozo buttons of large dimensions are rare.

VERNIS MARTIN

THE famous varnish called *vernis Martin* was not in fact invented by the Martin brothers, but by a certain Clement, a French painter, who introduced the process in Paris at the end of the seventeenth century. At that time European cabinet-makers were trying to imitate Chinese lacquer and many pieces of furniture and trinkets such as boxes, bodkins and even water-jugs came to be finished in *vernis Martin*. Buttons of this type are very rare and are most likely to have been made in Paris during the second half of the nineteenth century.

VIKING BUTTONS

VERY few Viking buttons have yet been found in excavations of ancient burial grounds, but the most interesting were found on Chapel Hill, Balladoole, Isle of Man, in 1946. They are in bronze and decorated with enamels in *champlevé* which, however, have lost their original colours. Of circular form, 3.5 cm. in diameter, they are domed with a milled edge. They are decorated with a cross and a very primitive spiral motif, similar to the enamelled objects of Ireland and Scotland of the ninth century. They are displayed in the Manx Museum.

Viking enamel buttons from the 10th century. Reproduced by permission of the Manx Museum, Douglas, Isle of Man.

WEDGWOOD BUTTONS

JOSIAH Wedgwood, the famous eighteenth-century Staffordshire potter and porcelain manufacturer, inventor of jasperware, received his first order for buttons from Matthew Boulton in 1773. The Birmingham novelty-maker wanted to use jasperware medallions to decorate bracelets, boxes, combs and buttons. Framed in steel, silver or gold, the Wedgwood jasperware buttons were soon being exported, particularly to France and Germany.

Josiah Wedgwood had made some buttons in salt-glazed earthenware as early as 1755. After he had perfected his jasperware, his small cameos and intaglios were sold to outsiders to be mounted in gold, silver, gilt and steel frames and sold as buttons. Wedgwood also himself sold 'finished buttons', which, instead of being moulded with the body, had shanks applied as a separate piece. Those buttons were of various shapes: round, oval, domed, square or octagonal. They all went out of fashion at the beginning of the nineteenth century. Jasperware buttons were manufactured again in the last decade of the nineteenth century. Wedgwood again produced a small quantity of buttons in bone china, all with floral centres and coloured borders, in the 1920s. He also produced jasperware buttons for American collectors in 1951.

Pair of beautiful 18th-century Wedgwood buttons in jasperware, probably mounted on metal frames by Matthew Boulton, of Birmingham. Reproduced by kind permission of Birmingham City Museums and Art Gallery.

Above and left: Three of six hunt buttons depicting horse studies. Produced at the Wedgwood factory of Etruria c.1790 in white Jasper with blue dip. Diameter: 1½ inches.

The horse studies were modelled for Josiah Wedgwood by Edward Burch in 1786—from designs executed for the potter by George Stubbs.

Below: Two Wedgwood buttons, produced c.1790. In Jasper mounted in gold these depict Hercules and Apollo.

WOODEN BUTTONS

BUTTONS have been made from every variety of wood for centuries and some are really beautiful. Most of those that collectors are likely to find today were made in the nineteenth and twentieth centuries. They are carved, painted, trimmed with escutcheons, inlaid or marqueted, and made in mahogany, sycamore, boxwood, and fruitwood, but it takes an expert to determine the variety of wood used. Lovely buttons in hand-carved sunwood were made in Indonesia, but some of the most beautiful hand-painted wooden buttons were made in the Belgian town of Spa in the second half of the nineteenth century (see p. 111) and in Mauchline, in Scotland, during the same period. The most attractive wooden buttons, much sought after by collectors, are those with silver or metal escutcheons, those inlaid with mother-of-pearl or metal, and those which are handcarved. During the twenties and the thirties, numerous cheap wooden buttons were made for children's clothes, sometimes painted with objects or well known figures such as Mickey Mouse. During the same period enormous wooden buttons, six or seven centimetres in diameter, were also produced, presumably to fasten overcoats.

Left: Carved wooden button in boxwood decorated with steel facets and crescents. Second half of 19th century.

Right: Carved wooden button of the Art Nouveau period.